The Philosophy of Literature

The Philosophy of Literature

—Four Studies—

Donald Phillip Verene

CASCADE *Books* • Eugene, Oregon

THE PHILOSOPHY OF LITERATURE
Four Studies

Copyright © 2018 Donald Phillip Verene. All rights reserved. Except for brief quotations in critical publications or reviews, no part of this book may be reproduced in any manner without prior written permission from the publisher. Write: Permissions, Wipf and Stock Publishers, 199 W. 8th Ave., Suite 3, Eugene, OR 97401.

Cascade Books
An Imprint of Wipf and Stock Publishers
199 W. 8th Ave., Suite 3
Eugene, OR 97401

www.wipfandstock.com

PAPERBACK ISBN: 978-1-5326-4173-2
HARDCOVER ISBN: 978-1-5326-4174-9
EBOOK ISBN: 978-1-5326-4175-6

Cataloguing-in-Publication data:

Names: Verene, Donald Phillip, 1937–, author.

Title: The philosophy of literature : four studies / Donald Phillip Verene.

Description: Eugene, OR : Cascade Books, 2018 | Includes bibliographical references and index.

Identifiers: ISBN 978-1-5326-4173-2 (paperback) | ISBN 978-1-5326-4174-9 (hardcover) | ISBN 978-1-5326-4175-6 (ebook)

Subjects: LCSH: Literature—Philosophy.

Classification: PN49 .V49 2018 (paperback) | PN49 .V49 (ebook)

Manufactured in the U.S.A.   09/10/18

In memory of
Samuel Moon
1922–2011
Poet and teacher of literature
at Knox College

Above all, literature keeps language alive as our collective heritage.

Umberto Eco, *On Literature*

The sole advantage in possessing great works of literature lies in what they can help us to become.

George Santayana, *Three Philosophical Poets*

Contents

Preface | ix

Introduction: The School of the Poets | 1
1 The Ethics of Immortality of Borges's *El inmortal* | 37
2 The Metaphysics of *Finnegans Wake* | 59
3 The Politics of *The People, Yes* | 81
4 The Phenomenology of *The Ship of Fools* | 103

Bibliography | 129
Index | 135

Preface

Words are the natural bodies of thought. The languages and literatures in which the words live are the tongue and heart of the humanities. Since the eighteenth century, philosophy has progressively attached itself to various fields of human knowledge and forms of culture. This conception of philosophy has resulted in a series of "philosophies of." Modern philosophy contains formulations such as the philosophy of science, philosophy of history, and philosophy of religion, and broader designations, such as philosophy of nature, philosophy of human nature, and philosophy of culture. These "philosophies of" assume a transcendental standpoint, as found in the Kantian conception of critique; their aim is to make explicit the presuppositions, principles, and methods that account for the possibility of their subject matters.

Thought of as one of these fields of "philosophies of," the philosophy of literature considers the question of what literature is and the place it occupies in the imagination. In addition to this transcendental inquiry into literature as a subject matter, philosophy realizes that it itself is a kind of literature. Philosophy exists only in and through its use of words. Philosophy is a linguistic art. Through its words, philosophy attempts to take thought to what is ultimate—to the really real, *to ontos on*, and to the greatest good, *summum bonum*. This linguistic journey is the center of speculative philosophy, as distinct from critical philosophy. The self-satisfaction of critical philosophy is disturbed by the speculative use of the mind's eye to apprehend the divine, the transcendent realm of ideas. The Socratic question, unlike the transcendental method, seeks the unseen in the seen.

The speculative imagination and the poetic imagination have a common origin in the mythic imagination, in the narratives from which all human culture arises. From the archetypal images in the primal myths come the words, customs, deeds, and laws of all the nations at war and in peace.

Preface

The images are the original orientations from which the divine, civil, and natural orders emerge. Without a comprehension of the myth, humanity has no basis from which to apprehend its own autobiography.

Put in James Joyce's terms, from litter comes letter comes literature. From literature comes philosophy, when the idea is extracted from the image. When putting ideas into words, philosophy pursues a speech of pure thought. The speech of pure thought remains an ideal. Philosophical speech still requires the image as a means to access the idea. In philosophical literature we find an abiding dialectic between image as the medium of the imagination and idea as the medium of reason. When the philosopher's reason forms itself in words, it finds itself among the etymologies and images that words bring with them. In using language the philosopher goes to school with the poet. Even when philosophical language is employed for the pure expression of arguments and conceptual analysis, metaphors and the images that accompany them are required to make the points asserted comprehensible. The reader may pass over the presence of the metaphors, but they are there, embedded in the text.

How are we to understand the relation of philosophy to literature? There are, I think, four ways in which we may answer this question. I intend these to be not a rigid classification but a general scheme. Philosophy may be brought into connection with literature in more than one of these ways at once. In the four chapters that follow, I wish primarily to align a single work of literature with each of these ways, without fully excluding the others.

First, we may think of a work of literature *as* a kind of philosophy. In such a work, philosophical thought is merged fully into its forms of literary expression such that the reader thinks both philosophically and poetically at the same time. In such a work the author has deliberately put the literary imagination in the service of philosophical thought. We find this union in many of Jorge Luis Borges's *Ficciones*. It is especially evident in *El inmortal* (*The Immortal*), which is the subject of chapter 1 of the present work.

Second, we may connect philosophy to literature in the specific sense of philosophy *of* literature. In such a connection, philosophy maintains its separate stance from the work of literature and becomes the means for comprehending it. Philosophy in this way brings its own interests to the literary work being interpreted, and in so doing we see the literary work in philosophical terms. Chapter 2 takes this approach to interpreting the intricate text of James Joyce's *Finnegans Wake*.

Preface

Third, we may connect philosophy to a work of literature by searching out philosophical ideas that happen to reside *in* it. The purpose in this connection of philosophy to literature is neither to approach a work of literature as a type of philosophizing nor to develop a comprehensive interpretation of it in philosophical terms. A work of literature is regarded as a source of ideas of philosophical interest: the divine, the self, and the world. The work is regarded not as particularly philosophical in form but as a repository of philosophical insights. Carl Sandburg's epic poem, *The People, Yes* is discussed from this perspective in chapter 3.

Fourth, we may place a work of philosophy in a dialectical relation to a work of literature such that we may speak of philosophy *and* literature. This approach places two particular works side by side, one philosophical and one literary. Each may illuminate the other. They are both concerned with the same theme but each takes it up differently. The reader is not on one side more than another, and can consider the theme from each direction. The two works form a pair, one enriching the other. Chapter 4 takes this approach by joining G. W. F. Hegel's *Phenomenology of Spirit* (*Phänomenologie des Geistes*) with Sebastian Brant's *Ship of Fools* (*Das Narrenschiff*). Such a pairing suggests a way of doing philosophy in which philosophy and literature function as companions in the larger project of humanistic thought.

The pages that follow take the form of an essay rather than a treatise. Should the reader find benefit in the views considered herein, my aim is fulfilled. In an area of thought dominated by fashionable doctrines of literary interpretation, doctrines of interpretation come and go, but the great and ingenious works of literature and philosophy stand always as before—permanent residents of our thought and imagination.

I am most grateful for those students, graduate and undergraduate, who have listened and responded to these philosophical views of literature in my courses over the past fifty years. Without the kindness of their audience I would not have had these thoughts.

I thank, once again, Molly Black Verene, for her transcription of my handwritten manuscript into a presentable, typed text, suitable for publication. May it be of interest to those who still practice the ancient art of reading books.

Introduction
The School of the Poets

Mythology and Poetry

R. G. Collingwood, in discussing the idea of philosophy as a branch of literature, declares: "the philosopher must go to school with the poets in order to learn the use of language."[1] We may add that not only must the philosopher go to school with the poets but all who wish to put thought into words must seek out the teaching of the poets, for the language of poetry is the first language of humanity. The poem points back to the original sense of speech—the expression of the world as felt. When we add, to this power, the power language has to explain the world, philosophy comes forth. Collingwood also says: "A philosophical work, if it must be called a poem, is not a mere poem, but a poem of the intellect."[2] The syllogism of the human psyche is composed of the passions and the intellect with the will as its middle term. To speak fully, that is, eloquently, is to join the passions with the intellect. The imagination and reason must be companions in the mind.

Within the imagination there are two senses of poetry—poetry as myth and poetry as myth remembered. Poetry as myth has no individual authorship. Poetry in this sense is composed of the original thoughts of a people, the form of their collective consciousness. Poetry as myth remembered is the product of an individual author. It is myth remembered in the sense that mythic thought supplies the archetypes on which the post-mythic poet

---

1. Collingwood, *Essay*, 214.
2. Ibid., 212.

draws to form images. A post-mythic poem affects us or fails to affect us, depending on whether it connects us with the archetypes. Mythic poetry is governed only by the trope of metaphor. It allows the peoples who produce it to bring the things of the world into existence and to see the similarities in the dissimilar, to live in a world that can be formed in the imagination and narrated.

In the *Enuma Elish*, Apsu (the ocean) and Tiamat (the primeval waters) join so as to produce the divine natural forces that bring the world into being.

> When there was no heaven,
> no earth, no height, no depth, no name,
> when Apsu was alone,
> the sweet water, the first begetter; and Tiamat
> the bitter water, and that
> return to the womb, her Mummu,
> when there were no gods—[3]

Post-mythic poetry adds to the metaphor the possibilities of the trope of irony. Irony allows for not just the coincidence of opposites but also for their juxtaposition as incongruities. The mythic mind is all-inclusive, but without the distance from the object that irony provides; the post-mythic mind can stand back from itself and experience the comic and the puzzling.

How does myth come about, and how does it differ from the rational? Myths are the first thoughts of humanity and are products of a primordial sense of speculative thought as it combines with the imagination. Speculative thought is a synonym for metaphysics. For metaphysical mentality the phenomenal world is primarily an "It." For mythic or archaic mentality the world is primarily a "Thou." The phenomenal world for the mythic mind is not a neutral object; it has the character of a personality, the actions of which are unpredictable. For the mythic mind nothing is inanimate. Myth is a form of poetry but, unlike poetry, the assertions of myth are categorical truths. Poetry or literature generally, in its formation of fictions, offers hypothetical truths. Myth will tell us of the nature of the true human beings. Non-mythic poetry can tell us of only various aspects of human life. A character in a play or a poem shows us one or more aspects of what it means to be human. But the myths of any archaic people present these people as the true human beings. All else are spirits, gods, demons, or animals.

---

3. Sproul, *Primal Myths*, 92.

Introduction

The distinction between subjective and objective knowledge is without meaning for the mythic mind. The human being, the world, and the gods are a continuum as expressed in this Mesopotamian incantation:

> Enlil is my head, my face is the day;
> Urash, the peerless god, is the protecting spirit leading my way.
> My neck is the necklace of the goddess Ninlil,
> My two arms are the sickle of the western moon,
> My fingers tamarisk, bone of the gods of heaven;
> They ward off the embrace of sorcery from my body;
> The gods Lugal-edinna and Latarak are my breast and knees;
> Muhra my ever-wandering feet.[4]

The self is in the world as it is in a dream. There is no distance from the object. Anything that has temporal or spatial congruence with another thing can be its "cause." The more "causal" connections one thing has with another, the richer is its reality. Rational mind classifies the world into types of objects such that only certain particular things can cause certain particular things that can be understood in terms of a specifiable principle. This sense of causality allows for the presence of accident. In the world of myth, nothing happens by accident. All that happens, happens for a "reason"; that is, all is the result of some will that is either sacred or profane, divine or demonic. When the mythic mind seeks to know why two things coincide, it looks not for a principle of "how" this event happens, but for "who" is its cause.

The mythic mind does not look for a single explanation of an event. The more one event can be connected to other events, the more being the event has. Each event has a personality with many sides. The phenomenal world is a drama. Time, for the mythic mind, is not a succession of events or moments. Time is understood in terms of an absolute division between the great time of origin, the time from which all things come, and the time of daily events of ordinary time. Myth is speech that embodies the meaning of ritual in language. Ritual and myth are a reenactment of the time of origin. The contact with origin makes the time of daily life tolerable.

Space for the mythic mind is not a continuum of "spaces." Space is ordered by the distinction between the sacred space of the center around which a people lives and which makes a connection between earth (the region of humans) and sky (the region of the gods) and profane space that radiates from the sacred center into the distance. Time and space are

---

4. Quoted in Frankfort, *Ancient Man*, 133.

qualitative, not quantitative. The social order replicates the natural order. For example, the mythic sense of the center is preserved in the inscription in the Roman Forum—*Curia umbilicus urbis Romae*—the Forum is the center of Rome, at the navel of the world. All primordial and ancient peoples live at the exact center, the navel, of the great body of the world.

For the mythic mind the past is absolute, the realm where all the ancestors dwell. The poetic mind appears in Greek thought from the mythic mind when Hesiod says that the Muses sing of what was, is, and is to come.[5] The past has a continuum with the present and the present has a continuum with the future. Moreover, Hesiod says, the Muses sing both true and false songs, but can sing true ones when they will. The distinction between true and false in the sense of truth and error is not a distinction within the mythic mind. A myth is *vera narratio*, a true narration. In this sense it is the thought of a perception or a feeling. A perception is always true; it is the apprehension of what is. To portray a perception as an image and then to expand the image into a narration, in the sense that every metaphor is a fable in brief, is simply to present a truth. A myth does not contain an internal dialectic between truth and error. What it says is what is.

With Homer we move from myth to poetry. Homer becomes the teacher of the Greek people. As such his poems instruct, and to be instructed is not simply to be presented with the way things are; it is to be shown the difference between what is wise and what is not. Achilles becomes the embodiment of the virtue of courage. Odysseus becomes the embodiment of prudence. They become guides to life. Poetry arises from myth as the counterpoint to science: the nature of Wordsworth is the counterpoint of the nature of Newton. Malinowski, in his little classic of anthropological literature *Magic, Science and Religion*, says that "every primordial community is in possession of a considerable store of knowledge based on experience and fashioned by reason."[6]

In practical activities such as crafts and agriculture, rules are employed that are rationally organized and empirically based. In planting crops the primordial community is well aware of the effects of soil conditions, weather, and pests, and in building canoes or dugouts, of the importance of proper materials, principles of stability, and hydrodynamics. The primordial farmer's or craftsman's knowledge is proto-scientific. The rules followed and communicated are a matter of experience not taken to the

---

5. Hesiod, *Theogony* 25.
6. Malinowski, *Magic, Science and Religion*, 26.

Introduction

level of theory. When the primitive islander is fashioning a canoe he can explain the need for an outrigger and necessary water displacement. But when asked what is the meaning of a ritual to launch the canoe in which it is connected to the forces of nature, the craftsman will reply that the elements of the construction of the canoe will protect it from the forces of the waves, but only when it is aligned with the universe by the ritual will it be protected from the danger of the great wave.

Ernst Cassirer, in his little classic of philosophy of culture *Language and Myth*, shows how language develops from its mythico-magical form in the image to its discursive power to abstract qualities from objects perceived and to build them into a classificatory scheme. Once this freedom from the concreteness of the image has been overcome, and language has grown into a vehicle of thought and become the expression of judgments and concepts, the wealth of immediate experience has been lost. In postmythic poetry, the original creative power of language is renewed and regenerated. Cassirer says: "Here it recovers the fullness of life; but it is no longer a life mythically bound and fettered, but an aesthetically liberated life. Among all types and forms of poetry, the lyric is the one which most clearly mirrors this ideal development."[7]

The lyric poetry of Hölderlin or Keats does not simply revert to the mythic order of the world and reinstate the world of gods and demons that hold the human spirit in their grasp. Poetry, and literature generally, present a world of fantasy and fiction in which the realm of pure feeling can be entered and expressed. The human spirit is not fettered by mythic forces but is liberated into a realm in which it can move in terms of its own volition without hindrance. In this realm of artistic making, the self can reveal itself to itself. It can be anything it wishes to be and in so doing it experiences freedom as self-determination. In poetry the spirit takes flight to its own destination. In this flight there is a parallel to the philosophy of Socrates's questioning, through which we allow thought to take us wherever the questioning leads without an answer predetermined.

Metaphysical philosophy and mythical thought share a beginning. Aristotle recognizes this in his passage in the *Metaphysics* concerning wonder (*thauma*): "For it is owing to their wonder that men both now begin and at first began to philosophize."[8] Wonder first occurs in response to specific difficulties (*aporiai*), then expands to the moon, the sun, and the stars and

---

7. Cassirer, *Language and Myth*, 98–99.
8. Aristotle, *Metaphysics* 982b.

from there to the genesis of the universe. Wonder both begins metaphysical speculation and continues it as thought increases its object of knowledge. Thought engages in *diaporia* as it explores various routes of investigation and dialectical considerations of opinions. Aristotle says: "even the lover of myth [*philomuthos*] is in a sense a lover of wisdom [*philosophos*], for myth is composed of wonders."[9] Philosophy and mythology, thus, have a common point of departure. But the philosopher's love of wisdom is pursued in terms of arguments or discourse (*logos*) and the perplexity that causes wonder occurs from "a state of equality between contrary reasonings," as Aristotle observes in the *Topics*.[10]

The lover of myth experiences *aporiai* on an existential level, not as a break in thought but as a break in being. The mythmaker does not experience being as the distinction between being *qua* being (*to on he on*), the object of metaphysics, and individual beings (*onta*), the objects of the particular sciences and fields of thought. For the primordial mind, an *aporia* is confronted by what the historian of religion Hermann Usener describes as *Augenblicksgötter*—"momentary gods"—involuntary formations envisioned on the spur of the moment. These deities are the oldest experience of mythico-religious consciousness. Regarding Usener's conception of these deities, Cassirer says: "These beings do not personify any force of nature, nor do they represent some special aspect of human life; no recurrent trait or value is retained in them and transformed into a mythico-religious image; it is something purely instantaneous, a fleeting, emerging and vanishing mental content, whose objectification and outward discharge produces the image of the 'momentary deity.'"[11]

These momentary deities come and go like subjective feelings but they are objectively apprehended as breaks in ordinary space and time. They are external encounters, not perplexities of thought. These momentary *aporiai* of feeling are overcome by the power of the imagination to transform the sun, the moon, and the stars and the genesis of the universe into images and these images into narrations. Mythic narrations maintain their truth by repetition. Myths, like musical pieces and like poems, are repeated over and over, each performance adding to the previous version. They each take us out of time. Myths are a circle in which what is portrayed comes back on itself. The symbols involved are presentational, not representational. They

---

9. Ibid.
10. Aristotle, *Topics* 145b.
11. Cassirer, *Language and Myth*, 17–18.

Introduction

do not refer to the world. They embody the world in their own immediacy. The world itself is sustained by them and its being is constantly renewed through them.

The primordial experience of *Augensblicksgötter*, literally, the appearance in the blink of an eye of a divine presence, is the origin of the sublime that is different from but associated with aesthetic perception. It is the primordial counterpart to the epiphany that can occur to the audience of a great oration or work of literature. This epiphany offers us a new sense of being, a new way of seeing. It takes us to a sense of the unseen that is at the basis of metaphor.[12] Like the momentary god it is the apprehension of a breakthrough, an *Einbruch* that transports the human spirit out of space and time to a sense of the *Jenseits*, the beyond, the unseen that is always more than the seen. It is the region of the Platonic forms and the Hegelian Absolute, what lies beyond Kantian Understanding and accounts for the human ability to grasp things as more than they appear. The aesthetic goes back to the mythic narration. The sublime goes back to what the aesthetic cannot reach but to which it can stand in relation—the divine itself. The aesthetic is not self-sufficient even though it is self-determinate. It requires the sublime to provide a sense of the beyond. The sublime is a sense of the ultimate, the unlimited—the *Unendlichkeit*—that appears within the limited.

The wonder that originates metaphysical philosophy and results in rational discourse seeks the real, in terms of a single unvarying account. Any metaphysics can be read and re-read, but the aim of the reading is always governed by the attempt to have coherence and consistency, to bridge the oppositions metaphysics confronts. In the myth there is no such concern. The lover of myth is attached to its images; they do not result in discourse or dialectical resolutions. The mythic narrative simply encompasses all oppositions in one way or another and leaves nothing intellectually resolved. The mythmaker and the myth teller produce an Aristotelian *catharsis*.[13] Emotions become objects apprehended—that are brought forth and confronted. What cannot be reached by thought is a wisdom of the passions. Metaphysical wonder results in curiosity, which drives the desire to know the world. But mythical wonder results in a release of passions, so as to feel the world in the image.

---

12. Ibid., 83–99.
13. Aristotle, *Poetics* 1449b.

Both metaphysics and myth aim at the complete speech. They attempt to put the world into language. Wonder, as Aristotle claims, leads ultimately to an account of the genesis of the universe. Myth is caught in the immediacy of the image, an immediacy from which there is no escape. Metaphysics, like art, is an activity of self-determination that overcomes immediacy and thus makes its truths as a series of freely taken acts.

The Platonic Quarrel

In the tenth book of the *Republic*, once the city in speech has been made, the Platonic-Socrates returns unexpectedly to the question of imitation (*mimesis*) that had been put aside in the discussion of the poets in Book 3. There the solution to the presence of the poet in the city—who would imitate all things without concern for what is proper as a subject of imitation and what is not—was to "send him to another city, with myrrh poured over his head and crowned with wool."[14] Such a poet would feel honored, for "we would fall on our knees before him as a man sacred, wonderful, and pleasing," but he would be surprised to discover himself outside the city walls, sent on his way to sing his words elsewhere.[15] For Plato, imitation is a form of deception or illusion, practiced by the poets in epic, tragic, comic, or dithyrambic speech.

The source for the view of imitation as deception (*apate*) may be Gorgias. Plutarch, in his essay on how to study poetry, says: "Gorgias called tragedy a deception."[16] Such deception, however, falls on deaf ears if its audience is one of witless and foolish persons. As Plutarch further reports, Simonides, when asked why the Thessalians were the only people whom he did not deceive, answered: "Oh, they are too ignorant to be deceived by me."[17] Recall Socrates telling Crito how foolish he would appear if he fled Athens in self-exile, to live roistering in Thessaly, an area too remote, and occupied by a population too disunited and witless, to play a role in Greek history.[18] An imitation, by definition, is not the real thing. Thus there is always something false about it. But the witless take all at face value and do not question the nature of what is before them.

14. Plato, *Republic* 398a.
15. Ibid.
16. Plutarch, *Moralia* 15d.
17. Ibid.
18. Plato, *Crito* 53d–54a.

Introduction

The claim that poetry deceives originates in the introduction of the Muses in Hesiod's *Theogony*, in which, as mentioned earlier, it is said they sing of what was, is, and is to come and that, in so doing, they can sing both true and false songs, but true songs when they will.[19] Among the Latins, Horace states that: "Most of us poets... deceive ourselves by the semblance of truth [*decipimur specie recti*]."[20] The poets deceive even themselves, for they know not the standard of truth. The inspiration of the Muses does not carry with it the criterion of how to distinguish between true and false songs. It is a secret kept by the Muses.

Something of this secret may be revealed by Aristotle's comment in the *Poetics*, that "Homer more than any other has taught the others the art of framing lies in the right way. I mean the use of paralogism."[21] The poet achieves the semblance of truth by presenting an occurrence in such a way that the audience assumes that if the latter is so, then the former must be so. Such reasoning is the so-called *fallacia consequentis*. It is false reasoning to infer, from the truth of the consequent, the truth of the antecedent. In a syllogism, if valid, the major and minor premises cannot both be false. But the truth of the conclusion in itself is insufficient to determine the validity of the syllogism. Put in another way, if p implies q, to affirm q does not establish the truth of p (the inversion of the argument form known as *modus ponens*). Poetry can make us put logic aside. As in any form of sophistical refutation, we may be led psychologically to accept what is logically unacceptable and unexpected (*paralogos*). The poet is not deliberately mendacious. The poet has license to go where logic does not go.

Aristotle inherits the term "imitation" (*mimesis*) from Plato, but regards the *techne* of poetry, that produces imitations, as an extension of the general human fascination and delight in the act of imitating. Human beings not only by their nature desire to know; they also desire to imitate: "Imitation is natural to man from childhood, one of his advantages over the lower animals being this, that he is the most imitative creature in the world, and learns first by imitation. And it is also natural for all to delight in works of imitation."[22] For Aristotle, imitation is part of human nature. His concern in the *Poetics* is to describe how to compose successful poems and to determine the sense in which poetry is among the productive sci-

---

19. Hesiod, *Theogony* 25.
20. Horace, *Ars poetica* 24–25.
21. Aristotle, *Poetics* 1460a.
22. Ibid. 1448b.

The Philosophy of Literature

ences. Aristotle can write the *Poetics* as he does because Plato has settled the quarrel between philosophy and poetry; philosophy and poetry can go their own ways. This allows Aristotle to place poetry within the general scheme of the sciences—theoretical, practical, and productive. Then, what is the quarrel? And how has Plato settled it?

Plato faces the question whether philosophers are a new school of poets or whether they are bringers of a new kind of knowing. Unlike the poem of Parmenides, or the metrical writing of Empedocles, the *Republic* is a complete speech in prose, like Plato's other major dialogues. It is Plato's intention to replace Homer's poems as the guide to Greek life with the process of rational speculation known to the "friends of the forms." To accomplish this separation, philosophy must be shown to be not simply different in degree but also in kind from poetry.

In the tenth book of the *Republic*, Plato considers this difference in two ways—in terms of knowing *that* and in terms of knowing *how*. He first considers the three senses of apprehending a couch—the form of a couch itself, that is made by a god, the particular couch made by a craftsman, and the image of a couch that is made by the poet or painter. The word involved in this threefold distinction is *poiein*, to make and to compose poetry. The philosopher knows that the being of the couch is the form (*eidos*, *idea*). The poet knows the couch to be what it is only in terms of its image (*eidolon*, *eikon*).

Plato then asks whether the poet has a knowledge of how something is used or done. A bridle is made by the leather worker, who cuts its pieces, and by the smith, who forges its metal parts. But they are not users of the bridle. The horseman knows how to use the bridle and how good or ill it is in its function of controlling the horse. The poet can portray the bridle and the painter can paint its picture but neither can use it; neither has a knowledge of how it functions or of its excellence in use. The same applies to the making and maintaining of a *polis*. Homer may portray kings and warriors, but there is no evidence that Homer or the poets that follow him have ever governed an actual state or led a military campaign. We can no more gain a knowledge of politics than a knowledge of horsemanship from Homer's poems.

We are deceived if we think we can learn the true nature of things from imitations or that we can learn successful conduct from the imitations of human actions. These are the central conclusions Plato has established. What Plato does not say, in this analysis, is that the philosopher makes

Introduction

neither the form of the couch nor the particular physical couch, nor does the philosopher make a poetic portrayal of the couch. Also, neither Homer nor the philosopher is a ruler of the *polis*. Plato's famous claim that, until philosophers become kings in their countries or kings take up the study of philosophy, no state can be properly ruled, is a claim of the highest improbability. It is an irony to have us realize that the love of wisdom and the love of politics cannot be combined.[23] Thus in the *Laws* Plato says that the city in speech of the *Republic* describes a state for the gods or the children of gods. It is a second, major, ironic claim.[24]

The unseen text of the tenth book of the *Republic* is the irony that both the poet and the philosopher are makers in words. They are both imitators, and this commonality is why the quarrel is so strong. Plato even declares the quarrel in an ironic manner, saying that we should tell poetry "lest it convict us for a certain harshness and rusticity, that there is an old quarrel between philosophy and poetry."[25] There may or may not really be an old quarrel. The poetic phrases that Plato then quotes are strange and unconvincing to verify such a quarrel. But we are at least certain that there now is a quarrel, to which Plato is a party. In a further irony Plato says he would be delighted to receive an apology from the poets to justify their activity and return from exile to a city of good laws. But, Plato says, should this speech not be forthcoming, we will chant our own argument to ourselves as a countercharm, lest the poets attempt to re-enter the city by appealing to our inborn love of poetry.[26]

The difference between poetic making and philosophic making is the object imitated. The poet imitates the visible object—the thing. The philosopher imitates the invisible object—the idea. Both the poet and the philosopher have only words at their disposal. The poet attempts to put the visible, what can be seen by the bodily eye, into words. The philosopher attempts to put the invisible into words, what can be seen by the mind's eye. The speech of the philosopher is an imitation of the world of forms. The poet's speech is fundamentally metaphorical, in that the metaphor allows us to visualize the similar in what otherwise appears dissimilar. Philosophical speech is

---

23. Plato, *Republic* 473c–d.
24. Plato, *Laws* 739d–e.
25. Plato, *Republic* 607a.
26. Ibid. 607c–608a.

fundamentally ironic, because the unseen can never appropriately, that is literally, be put into words. Speech falls short of expressing the Good.

As Plato makes clear in the *Seventh Letter*, nothing of his philosophy has been written down. "There is no writing of mine about these matters, nor will there ever be one. For this knowledge is not something that can be put into words like other sciences."[27] His teaching is transmitted as an intellectual fire that can leap between teacher and pupil. There are no words that can literally encompass the ultimate. Thus philosophic speech is inherently deceptive. Poetic speech is in competition with philosophic because it appears profound by being concrete and immediate. Philosophy always speaks beyond the image, beyond the concrete, and attempts to achieve concreteness by speaking of the whole. Philosophy is divine speech in that it imitates the god who is the maker of the forms. The philosopher imitates the god by re-making the forms in speech.

The Platonic dialogues are formulated from irony understood as a rhetorical figure, which is achieved by the expansion of irony as a trope to the motif of a life stance and mentality. Quintilian connects the meaning of *eironeia* with "dissimulation." He says that the trope of irony generally claims the opposite of what a statement literally means. But the trope of irony as such does not pretend something different. The rhetorical figure of irony does involve pretense, such that it can determine the entire shape of thought and its expression. Quintilian says: "Indeed a whole life may be held to illustrate Irony, as was thought of Socrates, who was called *eiron* because he played the part of an ignoramus, who marveled at the supposed wisdom of others. Thus, just as a continued series of Metaphors produces Allegory, so sustained use of the Trope Irony will give rise to the Figure."[28]

In his exchange with Socrates at the beginning of the *Republic*, Thrasymachus says: "Here is that habitual irony of Socrates. I knew it, and I predicted to these fellows that you wouldn't be willing to answer, that you would be ironic and do anything rather than answer if someone asked you something." Socrates immediately replies: "That's because you are wise, Thrasymachus."[29] In his encomium on Socrates in the *Symposium*, Alcibiades says that Socrates's "whole life is one big game—a game of irony."[30] He compares Socrates to a statue of Silenus, one of the satyr-like minor deities

---

27. Plato, *Seventh Letter* 341c.
28. Quintilian, *Institutio oratoria* 9.2.46.
29. Plato, *Republic* 237a.
30. Plato, *Symposium* 216e.

Introduction

and a companion of Dionysus, which has within it many tiny statues of the gods.[31] He says that Socrates's "ideas and arguments are just like those hollow statues of Silenus."[32] He says Socrates is always making the same arguments and always talking about ordinary things in ordinary or even coarse words. He says Socrates's speeches seem laughable. "But if you see them when they open up like statues, if you go behind their surface, you'll realize that no other arguments make any sense."[33] Alcibiades's speech on Socrates is perhaps the first full description of an individual in Greek literature, as the Greeks understood particular persons in terms of human types, not as unique personalities.

Irony is the philosopher's remedy against literal-mindedness. Hegel says: "Men without aesthetic sense are our literal-minded philosophers [*unsere Buchstabenphilosophen*]."[34] He says one cannot be ingenious (*geistreich*) or even argue well without aesthetic sense. Socrates's irony causes him to go about in a mask while always insisting that he is just what he is. The real Socrates is the unseen, like the images inside the statue, and the real Socrates can be seen, if it can be seen at all, by those who know how to listen to his arguments. Cassirer says that Socrates is the discoverer of philosophical irony. Socrates is also the discoverer of the question as the instrument of philosophy. Irony and the question combine in Socrates's way of thinking. Socrates defies classification, for it remains unclear whether he is essentially a theoretician or a practician—whether he belongs primarily to the sphere of seeking theoretical knowledge or is concerned only with practical action. Cassirer says: "As soon as we believe that we have grasped the 'true' face of Socrates and of Socratic thought, then this 'truth' dissolves. Our 'knowledge' is transformed into 'ignorance.' Socrates seems to defy every attempt to 'pin him down'; his every aspect turns into its opposite. This [is] a fundamental part of Socratic irony. This 'irony' has been borne out again and again in the historical interpretations of the figure of Socrates."[35]

Socrates introduced a new ideal of philosophical existence in his practice of ironical disguise. Once this sense of irony is understood, it determines the mentality and the manner of life of the philosophically educated. From Socrates, the philosopher can learn the logic of the mask. Once the

---

31. Ibid. 215b.
32. Ibid. 221e.
33. Ibid. 222a.
34. Hegel, "Systemprogramm," in *Werke*, 1:235. My translation.
35. Cassirer, *Philosophy of Symbolic Forms*, 4:184.

profundity of the Socratic irony is grasped, it is not possible to retreat to the refuge of literal-mindedness and the practice of critical thinking that accompanies it. Socratic irony guides him even at his death. How ironic it is for him to argue, on the day of his death, whether it is possible to prove the immortality of the soul, as related in the *Phaedo*. When Crito asks how they should bury him, Socrates replies: "In any way you like, if you can catch me and I do not escape you."[36] When his body is growing cold and stiff from the hemlock, Socrates uncovers his head and utters his last words: "Crito, we owe a cock to Asclepius, make this offering to him and do not forget."[37] He slips back under the blanket and is gone, passing away with this final irony. Asclepius, being the god of healing, relieves him of bodily life. A cock, with its feathers and beak, is the universal sign of the fool, and, as it is said earlier: "any man who faces death with confidence is foolish, unless he can prove that the soul is altogether immortal."[38] Socrates says he holds the soul to be immortal, but he does not claim to have altogether proved it. To sacrifice a cock to Asclepius is the least expensive sacrifice that one can make.

The poets offer us tragedy or comedy—the two faces on the masks on the cornice of the stage-opening of the theater—sadness and laughter. But the philosophers do not offer us the alternatives of a tragic or a comic sense of life. They offer us instead a tragicomic sense of life. Socrates is the comic figure who will talk to anyone, who professes ignorance, who has no regular employment, and who is a self-appointed gadfly of the state. At his trial he proposes that his penalty should be the right to be fed his meals at the city's expense at the Prytaneum, along with the Olympian victors.[39] Socrates is also the tragic figure, the "best among us," who is convicted on false charges—no witnesses were ever brought forward to testify that they were corrupted or exposed to irreligion by Socrates. He is the tragic figure of philosophy, brought down because of his inability to alter his commitment to the rational love of wisdom that ties him to the *elenchos*.

The philosopher, unable to be satisfied with the oscillation between tragic and comic, the dichotomy through which the poets appeal to the emotions, resorts to irony. Irony allows the philosopher to restrain the emotions to allow reason to come forth as the guide to life. Irony opens

36. Plato, *Phaedo* 115c.
37. Ibid. 118a.
38. Ibid. 88b.
39. Plato, *Apology* 36d.

Introduction

the path to raise questions and takes the philosopher from the unexamined life to the examined life. But in so doing the philosopher disturbs the city, because wisdom, not politics, becomes the ultimate object of a whole human existence. To turn philosophy to politics, in place of self-knowledge that the Delphic oracle directs, is to produce bad philosophy. The political life is a life of pretension and opinion, not irony and wisdom. Philosophy is neither tragic nor comic but is "tragi-comedic."

All of true philosophy is a series of footnotes to Plato, and all of Plato is a series of footnotes to Socrates and to the great discoveries of Socrates—of irony and the philosophical question. If we keep this in mind we shall be able to recognize philosophy that is speculative and pursues the vision of the divine, and distinguish it from philosophy that is merely reflective and critical, for this literal-minded philosophy is humorless. Finally, we will be able to see that "those who rightly philosophize are practicing to die [*hoi orthos philosophountes apothneskein meletosi*]."[40]

Ars Poetica, Ars Philosophiae

Horace says the purpose of poetry is to instruct or to delight or to move, that is, to be helpful to life.[41] We may say the same of philosophy. Any philosophy must instruct us, even if its instruction is simply to have us recollect what we have overlooked or forgotten about experience. It must delight us, for it is of the greatest importance that what is said is interesting and attractive to the mind. And it must move us, in the sense that it places us in a new position in life, such that we may see what before was unseen. Great works of philosophy, like great works of literature, cause us to approach the world differently than we did before reading them. Should it seem novel to speak of philosophy as an art, it is not novel but Socratic. Recall Socrates's comment to Cebes at the beginning of the *Phaedo*; after attempting briefly to write poetry to comply with his dream that he should practice and cultivate the arts, he concludes that his true calling is "to practice the art of philosophy, this being the highest kind of art [*mousike*]."[42]

Archibald MacLeish, in his rewriting of Horace's work in his poem "Ars Poetica," ends with the assertion that a poem should simply be.[43] A

---

40. Plato, *Phaedo* 67e3–4. My translation.
41. Horace, *Ars poetica* 333.
42. Plato, *Phaedo* 61a.
43. MacLeish, "Ars Poetica," 386.

poem is an ontological statement. Its meaning is its being. Its purpose is simply to be. Its reality is the "what is" that is being. The ultimate benefit we receive from poetry is a grasp of what is. We may say the same of philosophy. Any philosophy must confront us with the really real. Once we are so confronted, the three meanings Horace assigns to poetry follow on naturally, as an instruction for philosophical speech. The poem is just there, for us to read again. The poem is a circle, closed in upon itself; its end takes us back to its beginning. A philosophy is a circle, a complete speech; its verification does not lie outside itself. Any attempt to criticize a philosophy causes us to philosophize. Once we philosophize we are caught in the circle of philosophy itself and can never free ourselves from it. We can only be in its terms.

Ars philosophiae has four essential characteristics. First, philosophical thought, and hence its expression, must be musical. To be musical is to be dialectical. Hegel explains this musical sense of dialectic in terms of his doctrine of the "speculative sentence" (*speculativer Satz*). The "reflective sentence" formed by the Understanding, not by Reason, joins the subject to the predicate in terms of identity, resulting in a monotone of thought. The speculative sentence connects subject and predicate in a fashion similar to the opposition that occurs between meter and accent in rhythm. As Hegel says: "Rhythm results from the suspended middle and the combination of both."[44]

In the speculative sentence, the joining of the subject and predicate does not eliminate their difference; instead their unity emerges as a harmony in which the subject passes over into the predicate that expresses its meaning. Yet once the subject merges with the predicate, the predicate, to maintain its meaning, must pass back to its connection with the subject, and a new sentence thus emerges. In this movement thought is in harmony with itself. The self speaks to itself; substance becomes subject, the self always circling on itself, making its own reality from what appears as other to itself.

Second, philosophical thought and its expression must be poetic. The philosopher must be a master of metaphor, for, as Aristotle says: "The greatest thing by far is to be a master of metaphor. It is the one thing that cannot be learnt from others; and it is also a sign of genius."[45] Metaphor is the key to the imagination; it is the trope that supplies reason with its start-

---

44. Hegel, *Phenomenology*, 38. My translation.
45. Aristotle, *Poetics* 1459a.

Introduction

ing points, its *archai*, for it is a scandal to logic that it cannot produce its presuppositions by ratiocination. Metaphor requires memory, in the sense that from memory we draw forth two things that can be seen as having a commonality.

There is nothing in memory that is not first in perception, and to join these things a second sense of perception is required. This second perception is *ingenium* or ingenuity—the power to apprehend similarity in dissimilars. Ingenuity provides memory with a new object, a new *topos* for its treasure house. The metaphor, in the grasp of the philosopher, is the basis for the question. Once two memorial perceptions are joined in the bond that is metaphor, a question can be formed of the nature of their connection. From this, Socrates, the inventor of the question, can produce the *elenchos* that then becomes the medium of philosophical thought. Poetry is satisfied with the metaphor, but philosophy is not, yet it must engage metaphor as an essential moment of its thought.

Third, philosophical expression must employ the trope of irony. The trope of irony, when fully extended in philosophical thinking, produces the rhetorical figure of irony. Without the trope of irony combined with that of metaphor, nothing great can be said. They allow us to say what literally cannot be said. The trope of irony allows language to carry a double meaning. What would be simply a contradiction—an assertion and its opposite—when formed as an irony allows us to think double. Irony allows us to think something twice. For a double is not two separate things or it would not be a double. A double is one thing in two guises. Aristotle says: "but surely to be double and to be 2 are not the same; if they are, one thing will be many."[46]

A double is also not a duplicate; it puts a thing against itself so that we may see it differently. Once we have seen a thing through its opposite we can never see it literally. If all bad poetry is sincere, all bad philosophy also is sincere. The thinker who cannot command the trope of irony will retreat into sincerity to attempt to force us to accept the importance of what is claimed. The opposite of sincerity is not insincerity in philosophical expression; the opposite of sincerity is irony. All great truth is reached only by the ironic statement, for such truth requires the expression of the inexpressible. Language falls before itself. We know then that the love of wisdom has been taken to its limits.

Fourth, philosophical thought and its expression must be sublime. Poetry and philosophy are both ultimate activities of the human psyche

---

46. Aristotle, *Metaphysics* 987a.

The Philosophy of Literature

because they are both ways to glimpse the Absolute. Without the sense of the Absolute we have poetry or philosophy that is simply sincere. The Absolute provides the element of the sublime. Sublime thought and expression take us elsewhere from ourselves. They relieve us of the world of the political, of the earthbound, the dullness inherent in critical thinking, and reason dedicated solely to the practical. Hegel says: "the owl of Minerva begins its flight only with the falling dusk."[47] The heavens are the region of the Absolute, that which is a reality seen from earth but wholly transcendent of it. Longinus says: "the Sublime consists in a consummate excellence and distinction of language, and that this alone gave to the greatest poets and prose writers their preeminence and clothed them with immortal fame. For the effect of genius is not to persuade the audience but rather to transport them out of themselves."[48] Philosophy, not motivated by the presence of the Absolute, may make its points gradually emerge from the whole course of its exposition, but "a well-timed flash of sublimity shatters everything like a bolt of lightning and reveals the full power of the speaker at a single stroke."[49]

Philosophical writing need not be beautiful, and it often is not. Should philosophical writing be beautiful it is all to the good. But above all it must be sublime, it must at some point provide the reader with epiphany, a moment in which the mind's eye sees what has been unseen. In this moment the reader becomes a friend of the forms. It takes many words to provide this second sight, but its occurrence makes all the reading of these words a Bacchanalian revel that has now become a scene of transparent, unbroken calm. The *thauma* of which Aristotle speaks is now known.[50]

Language is the master key to the human world. It is the agency of memory, as each word carries with it its own memory as its etymology. When language is constrained, the fullness of memory is constrained, and hence the fullness of human life itself. We find Socrates making this point in the final hour of his life, when he says to Crito: "Dear Crito, you know well, that to use words badly, is not only a misuse of language, it causes some harm to the soul."[51] Education is memory. To be learned is to be able to bring forth at the proper moment what has been said in the past.

---

47. Hegel, *Philosophie des Rechts*, in *Werke*, 7:28. My translation.
48. Longinus, *On the Sublime* 1.3.
49. Ibid. 1.4.
50. Aristotle, *Metaphysics* 982b.
51. Plato, *Phaedo* 115e. My translation.

Introduction

Learning is sublime, for, like Longinus's thunderbolt, by its means we can place something of the moment in a total perspective. What is otherwise momentary is enriched by recollection, the recollection of what has been thought before by humanity.

To express oneself well requires that we study beautiful speech by the poets and sublime speech by the philosophers. We require both the art of poetry and the art of philosophy. Between these two lies all that we need for eloquence. Eloquence, as Cicero and Quintilian have explained and as the Renaissance Humanists such as Leonardo Bruni and Giovanni Pico della Mirandola, as well as Giambattista Vico understood, is to speak fully and completely on a subject. Quintilian says that the verb *eloqui* means the communication of all the speaker has conceived. Without this power, he says, oratory is "useless, like a sword that is put up and will not come out of its scabbard."[52] Wisdom is a knowledge of things divine and human, a knowledge of the whole, and eloquence is to put the whole into words, as "wisdom speaking" (*la sapienza che parla*). We must experience eloquence to be eloquent, and that can be acquired only by the study of the canon. The canon is the memory of the learning of humanity and the source of learned memory for the individual. Without command of some significant portion of the canon we are without the ability to interpret ourselves, to see with our mind's eye what the mind's eye of humanity has seen.

Reading the canon is a denial of time, as the act of reading itself is such a denial. The everyday time of ordinary life in which one moment passes into the next can produce no meaning. Reading, like memory, interrupts this incessant passage of moments. To read is an activity of transcendence that allows us to suspend this ordinary time and enter into a world of the idea and the image. When we re-enter ordinary time we are armed with memory, with the permanence of thought that always awaits us in the great works. The authors of the great works are always there, like the ancestors who, in mythical time, exist at the edge of the world and look down upon us. It is through eloquence that we go to the edge of the world and think outside of time.

The necessity of this passage outside of time is what Niccolò Machiavelli knew, in his exile to his farm outside of Florence, and which he expresses in his famous letter to his benefactor Francesco Vettori, describing his life there. Machiavelli says: "On the coming of evening, I return to my house [having, even during the day in the fields, taken in his pocket works

---

52. Quintilian, *Institutio oratoria* 8.pr.15–16.

of Dante or Petrarca or Ovid] and enter my study; and at the door I take off the day's clothing, covered with mud and dust, and put on garments regal and courtly; and reclothed appropriately, I enter the ancient courts of ancient men, where received by them with affection, I feed on that food which only is mine and which I was born for, where I am not ashamed to speak with them and to ask them the reason for their actions; and they in their kindness answer me; and for four hours of time I do not feel boredom, I forget every trouble, I do not dread poverty, I am not frightened by death; entirely I give myself over to them."

Machiavelli then adds: "And because Dante says it does not produce knowledge when we hear but do not remember, I have noted everything in their conversation which has profited me."[53] This reading, he says, is the basis of his writing, the outcome of which is one of the most widely read and controversial books of the Western canon—*The Prince*.

The art of reading is the basis of the art of writing. Without reading, writing is just placing words on a surface, a practical act. Reading and writing, driven by the aim of eloquence, are the most impractical of acts, for their purpose is just themselves. Style is the ultimate aim of the educated mind. Expression that has less than this aim, unless it is just a matter of the relay of practical matters, does some harm to the soul. Real reading and real writing take the psyche into itself and give it inner form, by means of which it confronts the world, and we may say the same of real speaking, what the ancients knew as *ars oratoria*.

In his lectures on aesthetics, Hegel says that the Greeks "in the poems of Homer have a poetic bible."[54] The St. Louis Hegelians, one of the first philosophical movements in America, contemporary with the New England Transcendentalists, but preceding the pragmatism of James and Dewey, extended the principle of Hegel's view of Homer so as to formulate a canon. They saw literature as an art form that embodies the progressive self-realization of Absolute Spirit as a complement to the awareness of the Absolute in the philosophical pursuit of self-knowledge. One of their exponents, Denton Snider, spoke of the four literary bibles of the West; he saw them as reflecting the great drama of Absolute Spirit as it occurs in the drama of the cosmos. These bibles were the *Iliad* and *Odyssey* of Homer, the *Divine Comedy* of Dante, the plays of Shakespeare, and Goethe's *Faust*.[55]

---

53. Machiavelli, *Chief Works*, 2:929.
54. Hegel, *Ästhetik*, in *Werke*, 15:33. My translation.
55. De Armey and Good, eds., *St. Louis Hegelians*, 3:xxii.

Introduction

We may couple the art of poetry they exemplify with the art of philosophy as represented by figures that can be associated with them. Homer begins the story of Odysseus with the words: "Sing to me of the man, Muse, the man of twists and turns driven time and again off course, once he had plundered the hallowed heights of Troy [*Andra moi ennepe, Mousa* . . .]."[56] From the *Odyssey* we see life as a journey that, guided by our ingenuity, can take us to Ithaca and to the peace that it provides. Plato concludes the *Republic* with the description of the journey of the souls in the afterlife by saying: "And so here and in the thousand year journey that we have described we shall fare well [*eu prattomen*]."[57] What we must keep before us for life's journey that Odysseus teaches is prudence (*phronesis*), the power of reason to take us through any situation we face. What we must keep before us for our journey in life, as well as in the afterlife, from which, according to the Myth of Er, we will be reborn, that Plato teaches is *noesis*, the power to apprehend the forms that are governed by the Good. We will fare well in the sense of acting successfully, guided by our ability to do what is good. Reason will take us to *sophia* and give us the peace necessary to the virtuous life, such that, as Socrates says, no harm can come to a good man (*anthropos*). The reader of Homer and Plato is instructed twofold in what is needed for life's journey.

Dante begins the *Divine Comedy* with the lines: "Midway in the journey of our life I found myself in a dark wood, for the straight way was lost [*Nel mezzo del cammin di nostra vita mi ritrovai per una selva oscura, che la diritta via era smarrita*]."[58] The *selva oscura* is the earthly condition of the journey of life that must be overcome by the apprehension of the mount of joy, the *dilettoso monte*, the vision of divine peace that must direct our journey and offer us the standard of happiness, the life of contemplation. Giambattista Vico, in presenting the principles of his *New Science*, says: "In the night of thick darkness [*densa notte di tenebre*] enveloping the earliest antiquity, so remote from ourselves, there shines the eternal and never failing light [*lume eterno*] of a truth beyond all question: that the world of civil society has certainly been made by men, and that its principles are therefore to be found within the modifications of our own human mind."[59] He says to the reader: "O reader, that these proofs [*argomenti*] are of a kind

---

56. Homer, *Odyssey* 1.1.
57. Plato, *Republic* 621d.
58. Dante, *Inferno*, canto 1.2–3.
59. Vico, *New Science*, par. 331.

divine and should give thee a divine pleasure [*un divin piacere*], because in God knowing and making are one and the same."[60]

When we seek the origin of the journey on which we find ourselves we perceive its obscurity, yet at the same time we perceive the eternal light by which we can penetrate it. Once we see how to illuminate this dense night of origin from which the human world has emerged we will experience the divine pleasure comparable to Dante's glimpse of the mount of joy that motivates and guides his journey.[61] The reader is left with Dante's journey into the *Inferno*, *Purgatorio*, and *Paradiso*, and Vico's journey into the "ideal eternal history" (*storia ideal eterna*) that governs the common nature of the world of the nations. The reader of Dante and of Vico takes these two journeys and, like Dante, emerges with his desire and his will revolved "like a wheel that is evenly moved, by the Love which moves the sun and the other stars."[62] Like Vico, the reader emerges from the nightmare of history with the knowledge "that this Science carries inseparably with it the study of piety, and he who is not pious cannot be truly wise."[63] Dante offers us the peace of the soul that joins desire to will, and Vico offers the corresponding peace of the mind that joins piety with reason.

Perhaps the most famous line in the Shakespearean plays—a line everyone has heard—is that of Hamlet: "To be, or not to be; that is the question: Whether 'tis nobler in the mind to suffer the slings and arrows of outrageous fortune, or to take arms against a sea of troubles, and, by opposing, end them."[64] These lines step out from the play and raise in themselves the question of human existence. Do we accept our lot, the condition in which we find ourselves on life's journey? Should we meet our particular human condition with stoicism? Or should we attempt with all our powers to confront our troubles, to take whatever risks necessary to dominate the situation in which we find ourselves? Should we confront the "arrows of outrageous fortune"? It is a question of the self's relation to itself and to the world, put forward by the genius of Shakespeare in a single thought. We reason with ourselves, but it is a reasoning that repeats itself with each *aporia* we encounter on the journey of life. It tells us that fortune plays a role. To live is to confront the Fates (*Moirai*)—Lachesis, who holds sway

60. Ibid., par. 349.
61. Dante, *Inferno*, canto 1.77.
62. Dante, *Paradiso*, canto 33.144–45.
63. Vico, *New Science*, par. 1112.
64. Shakespeare, *Hamlet*, in *Complete Works*, act 3, scene 1, lines 57–62.

Introduction

over the past, Clotho, who holds in her grasp the present, and Atropos, who presides over the inevitable of the future. They are the logic of the Muses.

If, beside this sense of human existence, we put the logic of Bacon in his *Novum Organon*, a contrasting view of the self's relation to itself and the world appears. Bacon's new instrument is summarized in his famous assertion: "Human knowledge and human power meet in one; for where the cause is not known the effect cannot be produced. Nature to be commanded must be obeyed; and that which in contemplation is as the cause is in operation as the rule."[65] We obey nature in order to command nature: *Natura enim non nisi parendo vincitur*. The self now has a concept of itself as dedicated not simply to being in the world, but to forming the object of its interest according to its own desire. The question of how we should be or whether we should be is transcended by our power to make the object an item at our disposal. The twists and turns of Odysseus, guided by his prudence, are now transformed into the operation of a rule. Prudence is reason applied to the particular and its probabilities. The Baconian logic of induction, while yielding only probable knowledge of causes, aims at the reduction of the particular to the universality of the rule. The Baconian self is an active agent; it has put the instruction of the Delphic oracle aside.

Goethe's opening speech for Doctor Faustus is: "I have, alas, studied philosophy, Jurisprudence and medicine, too. And, worst of all, theology with keen endeavor, through and through – And here I am, for all my lore, The wretched fool I was before [*Habe nun, ach! Philosophie, Juristerei und Medizin und leider auch Theologie durchaus studiert mit heißem Bemühn. Da steh ich nun, ich armer Tor! Und bin so klug als wie zuvor*]."[66] To know is to traverse the encyclopaedia of the sciences. Knowledge is erudition; yet to what end? Such learning leaves life to itself; there is no theory that will tell the self what the human is. Each field has its own theories of its subject matter. But there is no theory of self-knowledge. Something else is required that lies outside the curriculum. The journey of life goes on despite the presence of these fields of knowledge. Each of these fields stands alone with its own standards of validity. The learner wanders through them as in an *ingens silva*, a vast forest of learning with no visible center or clearing. The traveler through this great forest finds no sense of direction that can establish the true path from the false.

---

65. Bacon, *Novum Organon*, in *Works*, 4:47.
66. Goethe, *Faust*, 92; lines 354–59.

The Philosophy of Literature

If we turn to Hegel's great *Bildungsroman* of the *Phenomenology of Spirit*, we find that the problem lies with our reliance on the Understanding (*Verstand*), for, as Hegel says, "a table of contents" is all the Understanding offers.[67] We are wandering through an *Inhaltsanzeige*, finding one subject after another. What we have forgotten is the fact that true knowing is the apprehension of the whole. Hegel says: "The True is the whole [*Das Wahre ist das Ganze*]. But the whole is nothing other than the essence of things, consummating itself through its development in them. We may say of the Absolute that it is essentially a *result*, that only in the *end* is it what it truly is."[68]

The Absolute is substance become Subject. Once the knowing self sees the Absolute not as a substance that supports all things by underlying them, it realizes that underlying all things is the human spirit (*Geist*) which develops itself as Subject knowing itself as a whole. Its stages, in accomplishing this Absolute knowing, is the self-determination of Reason. Knowledge of the True is not what the Understanding gives. For it, to know is to engage in criticism, claiming a standard to distinguish truth from error. This critical thinking is the domain of the individual sciences as opposed to the "science of the experience of consciousness." It is the True that we seek, not specific truths. For this we require a grasp of the whole. Our journey to the whole is a "highway of despair" (*Weg des Zweifels*), but the end of this way is the Absolute that brings with it the peace we seek through our attachment to Reason.

The Absolute is the point of divine pleasure the knower seeks. Yet it is easy to forget the whole and to be drawn from its illumination back into the forest of the sciences where, to apply Virgil's phrase: "we wander ignorant of the men and the places [*Ignari hominumque locorumque erramus*]."[69] The peace of mind of the Absolute, as the speech of Faust now warns us, is not easy to sustain. The philosopher is a stranger in a strange land. True philosophy requires us to cultivate the power of recollective memory (*Erinnerung*), for it is this power that keeps the whole—the flower of wisdom—in view.

---

67. Hegel, *Phenomenology*, 32.
68. Ibid., 11.
69. Virgil, *Aeneid* 1.332–33. My translation.

Introduction

The Study of Literature

The study of literature, as shown above, requires the idea of a canon. There are two canons: the Western canon and the Eastern or Asian canon. The Western canon begins with Homer's *Iliad* and *Odyssey*. "Iliad" as a word means simply a poem about Ilium. And the "Odyssey" (*Odusseia*) means simply the story of Odysseus. Through these two poems Homer became the teacher of the peoples of ancient Greece. The Eastern canon begins with the *I Ching or Book of Changes*. As Richard Wilhelm points out: "The Book of Changes—*I Ching* in Chinese—is unquestionably one of the most important books in the world's literature. Its origin goes back to mythical antiquity, and it has occupied the attention of the most eminent scholars of China down to the present day."[70]

The *Iliad* and *Odyssey* are the oldest known books of Western literature. All of European and Anglo-American culture is inconceivable without them. The philosophies of Plato and Aristotle cannot be comprehended without a grasp of their background in Homer. The *I Ching*, the "I" referring to "change" and "ching" meaning book, is the oldest book in world literature. The two branches of Chinese philosophy, Confucianism and Taoism, have their common root in this book. The idea of a canon is inseparable from the idea of origin. All books are about other books, implicitly or explicitly. The poems of Homer are the production of the mind of the Greek peoples themselves, and in this way become the first books. The linear signs of the *I Ching* are of such antiquity that they antedate historical memory and are attributed to the legendary figure Fu Hsi. The formation of the book into sixty-four hexagrams is attributed to King Wên, the progenitor of the Chou dynasty, and the texts affixed to the individual lines were added by his son, the Duke of Chou. It was in this form that Confucius encountered it and studied it.

Once the origin is established, the canon can go forward. Tradition constructs the canon for us as readers. Deriving from the Latin term, *traditio*, a giving over by means of words, an instruction, tradition is a transmission of knowledge and institutions through successive generations. We inherit the canon of great books of literature, philosophy, religion, and history. The canon we come upon is a great memory theater of ideas, images, interpretations, and insights. As we absorb the contents of this theater through reading the books that define it, we achieve an education in the

---

70. Wilhelm, *I Ching*, xlvii.

The Philosophy of Literature

Greek sense of *paideia* or the German sense of *Bildung*. We form our selves as part of the collective of human culture that has gone before us and is now passed on to us in words. The canon is not exhausted or closed off by any one list of books that may form it. Yet the canon is there as the principle that some books present us with the inner form of the human condition more than others.

A great book is a book of wisdom. A book of wisdom is one that in some way presents us with the whole of things, or that, thinking from it, we acquire the perspective from which we may see the whole of things. The basis for the canon so conceived is a repository of aesthetic, spiritual, intellectual, and imaginative excellence. The presence of these qualities provides the depth of these works. Their depth is the result of genius. Such books bring with them their own standard that over time is recognized, and the reader is led to them by a piety to tradition. A great book can be read by an indefinite number of readers and read by a single reader an indefinite number of times, without having the meaning it contains diminished. The opposite is the case with lesser books. Each time the great book is read it will yield new meanings and new possibilities of thought for the reader.

It is said, rightly, that those in philosophy should read Plato through every year. The Scriptures are inexhaustible. It is told that Confucius said if he had more years to live he would spend them on the *I Ching*. No real reader reads Dante or Shakespeare only once. We turn to the great historians time and again to confront the past. There are important and interesting works to read that supply specific ideas or views but they do not contain the human spirit in the unique way great books do. On a second reading of less than great works we come away with largely what we found on the first. We find things of definite interest in less than great books but they do not take us out of ourselves.

I do not intend my distinction between the Western and Eastern canons to be rigid. If to some extent these canons are merged we have a canon of world literature. We can see the dimensions of this world canon by looking to a list of ancient and early works. Such a list includes, in addition to those works just mentioned, *The Hebrew Bible and New Testament, Al-Qur'an, Bhagavad-Gita, Egyptian Book of the Dead, Analects, Tao tê Ching, Lankavatara Sutra, Gilgamesh, The Thousand and One Nights, The Rubaiyat,*

Introduction

Prose Edda and *Poetic Edda*, *Beowulf*, *Nibelungenlied*, and so on. There is no one canonical list upon which all will agree, but some argument may be possible regarding the importance of first and early books, those that have most firmly held their own in the workings of tradition. The ideal of the canon is a matter of learned discussion; that is its value.[71] There is no need to claim a final and fixed list. The closer in time works are to us, the less tradition can form the canon and the more learned preference sets a standard. There is no tradition of the recent past, the present, or the future. But the idea of the canon keeps us reading in order to seek out those works in which lie greatness and genius.

The canon of great books carries with it an education in taste, that sense or sentiment that has roots in the Renaissance and is solidified in the aesthetics of the eighteenth century. The Latin phrase *de gustibus non est disputandum* need not imply a relativism of taste, in the sense that there is no accounting for taste, that taste is totally subjective. Taste as a philosophical concept is a standard of excellence. The great ideas taken from the great books give the individual an intellectual and an aesthetic standard. It is a standard shared with the other readers of such books. To have taste is to have something that not everyone has. It is close, I think, to what A. N. Whitehead means by the sense of style. Whitehead says: "Style, in its finest sense, is the last acquirement of the educated mind; it is also the most useful. It pervades the whole being."[72] Style, as Whitehead says, is the ultimate morality of mind. Taste and style require the study of literature and the study of culture. To settle for anything less than the ideals of taste and style is a mistake that will go uncorrected for a lifetime.

There is another view of the idea of a canon that comes forth through the critical attack on the view just presented. Those who attack the idea of the canon usually direct their criticism toward the Western canon, with little or no awareness of the Eastern canon, held in high regard by the Asian cultures. The adherents of this view may be characterized as advocating a canon of *ressentiment*, to use Nietzsche's term.[73] The basis of the canon of resentment is not aesthetic, spiritual, intellectual, or imaginative excellence. It is political and ideological. The canon as it comes to us from tradition is deconstructed. The great books passed on to us by tradition are seen as fronts for class, gender, and racial prejudice. The Western canon, and

---

71. For a version of the works in the canon see Bloom, *Western Canon*, 531–67.
72. Whitehead, *Aims of Education*, 12.
73. Nietzsche, *Genealogy*, 36–39; see also Bloom, *Western Canon*, 15–41.

presumably the Eastern canon as I have described it, are to be replaced by a reading list of works that have been excluded by tradition from our attention—or perhaps there is to be no canon at all. Thus one book is as good as another, whatever one may find congenial.

This approach allows for a politically governed canon to be established on the basis of "critical thinking" or for a personal canon to reign in terms of those writers one happens to prefer over others. This second possibility comes close to doing away with reading at all in favor of exposure to views of the moment. Media over contemplation. The canon of resentment is fully intolerant of the canon of great books. They are by and large not to be read. But the adherent of the canon of great books is not intolerant of the books of the canon of resentment. These books have points to make of interest, but they do not offer a way to respond to the inscriptions on the *pronaos* of the temple of Apollo at Delphi: *gnothi seauton* and *meden agan*. Self-knowledge and moderation or the Taoist way and its power (*tê*) and the Confucian doctrine of the mean offer us a path to pursue the Socratic problem of whether we are a beast like Typhon or one of a gentler, more divine nature.[74]

The canon of the great books inspires us as human beings. The canon of the books of resentment inspire us as political beings of a particular type—those that would change social conditions but in so doing would avoid the Socratic question of their own being. The changes in the ways of the world that are advocated are often cosmic, but fleeting. In politics, nothing lasts. There is some of the Stoic in every true philosopher. The philosopher's approach to the study of literature is not that of the political reformer or moralist. It is the search for self-knowledge, the education of memory and imagination that can take us to the contemplative life of which Aristotle speaks: "So for one who is living, when his action is taken away, and, still more, his making something, what remains except contemplation? As a result, the activity of the god, because it is superior in blessedness, would be contemplative. And so in the case of the human activities, the one that is most akin to this would be most characterized in happiness [*eudaimonia*]."[75]

The reader of the canon of great books acquires an education in the Good, the True, and the Beautiful, and does this, to a large extent, through the poems, plays, novels, and narratives connected to metaphysics and

---

74. Plato, *Phaedrus* 230a.
75. Aristotle, *Nicomachean Ethics* 1178b.

Introduction

moral philosophy and to the deeds, languages, customs, and laws narrated by the historians. The adherent of the canon of resentment regards its works as instruments for the pursuit of a political agenda in which the individual self loses itself in the process of righting wrongs. No more can be said of this canon.

The literary fictions of the canon of great books take the reader from the world of probabilities to a world of certainties. It is a matter of probability whether the Trojan War actually occurred and whether it occurred on the site Schliemann discovered. But it is certain that Achilles, son of Peleus and Thetis, grandson of Aeacus, killed Hector with his bronze spear, aided by Athena, in Book 22 of the *Iliad*.

It is a matter of probability whether Dante met Beatrice first as a child in her family's garden, and later, as an adult, he followed her through the streets of Florence. But it is certain that Dante meets Beatrice in Canto 30 of *Purgatorio*, where she addresses him by name and prepares him to be guided into *Paradiso*.

It is a matter of probability what Caesar's last words were when he fell to a conspiracy led by Brutus and Cassius, on the Ides of March, and died at the foot of Pompey's statue. But it is certain that his last words in Act 3, scene 1 in *Julius Caesar* were: "Et tu Brute?"

It is a matter of probability to what extent Goethe intended the character of Faust to correspond to the historical figure in German culture. But it is certain that Mephistopheles appears in Faust's study, announced by the agitation of Faust's poodle, causing Faust to exclaim: "Das also war des Pudles Kern! [Then this was our poodle's core!]."[76]

As writers on the art of poetry from Aristotle to Horace insist, it is necessary that what occurs in fiction is probable. If not, the fiction fails. But unlike the probability that persists regarding the status of actual events, once the event is recorded in the fiction, it remains certain. The certainty that the imagination attains in the fiction is the prototype for the certainty sought in logical deduction.

As discussed earlier, the poet can go where logic cannot, and convince by means of paralogism, by inverting *modus ponens*. But the poem can also be a form of *modus ponens* that is done through concrete images. In the poem all must be present and interconnected, each element supporting the others: sound, syntax, structure, sense. Because we can grasp order in

---

76. Goethe, *Faust*, line 1323.

poetic form, we can grasp order in logical form. Poetry is presupposed by logic.

A grasp of Paul Verlaine's words, which begin with an epigraph of Arthur Rimbaud: "Il pleut doucement sur la ville," taking us to: "Il pleure dans mon coeur comme il pleut sur la ville [It rains tears in my heart as it rains on the town],"[77] forms thought in such a way that it can grasp a deductive order of propositions. If it rains on the town, then it rains in my heart. It rains on the town, thus it rains in my heart. Here we find agreement between poetic and logic.

In the development of mind, the similes of mythic poetry precede the comparisons of ratiocination. Historical narrative develops from both, in that historical thought requires palingenesis, in which events are reimagined in terms of a logical order so that we grasp their causes both natural and moral and the occasions of fortune. The study of literature allows us to pass back and forth from the poetic to the philosophic to the philologic or historic. The ability to move the mind's eye in this way is the master key to humanistic learning that results in the educated individual. This is also true of education in jurisprudence, for the forensic orator must be prepared to draw on a full range of human learning to bring the hearers to a grasp of the meaning of a particular point. Civic life, bereft of the inheritance of humanity, bereft of what is taught in the school of the ages, is a paltry thing. Literature and logic are what we need for speech that goes beyond the practical and ordinary.

Leonardo Bruni, in his letter on the study of literature addressed to Lady Battista Malatesta of Montefeltro, concludes his survey of the various forms of literature: "In sum, then, the excellence of which I speak comes only from a wide and various knowledge. It is necessary to read and comprehend a great deal, and to bestow great pains on the philosophers, the poets, the orators and historians and all the other writers. For thus comes that full and sufficient knowledge we need to appear eloquent, well-rounded, refined, and widely cultivated. Needed too is a well-developed and respectable literary skill of our own. For the two together reinforce each other and are mutually beneficial."[78] Eloquence is the skill to put the whole that is wisdom into words.

We can only anticipate becoming eloquent if we have immersed ourselves in modes of eloquent writing and speaking. "Literary skill without

---

77. Verlaine, "Il pleure dans mon coeur," in *Anthology*, 92.
78. Bruni, "Study of Literature," 123.

Introduction

knowledge is useless and sterile; and knowledge, however extensive, fades into the shadows without the glorious lamp of literature. Of what advantage is it to know many fine things if one has neither the ability to talk of them with distinction or write of them with praise? And so, literary skill and factual knowledge are in a manner of speaking wedded to each other."[79] Bruni says that this union of literary skill and factual knowledge (*scientia rerum*) is responsible for our admiration of the ancients, especially Plato, Democritus, Aristotle, Theophrastus, Varro, Cicero, Seneca, Augustine, Jerome, and Lactantius. We cannot decide, he says, whether it is their literary power or their knowledge that accounts for their glory, but either causes us to hold them and their works in memory.

Bruni says that in our study of literature and pursuit of eloquence we should have a focus: "It is religion and moral philosophy that ought to be our particular studies."[80] Bruni connects religion as a field of study with one of the five fields of the Humanists' *studia humanitatis*. This connection echoes the definition of wisdom as knowledge of divine and human things. Moral philosophy has at its center *phronesis* or prudence, and this knowledge of the human world is to be connected with *sophia*, the object of contemplative thought (*theoria*). Wisdom is a dialectic between the two that causes the self to extend its inner form in both directions.

What is the education that the study of the great books gives? From the study of the poets we learn the nature and the power of metaphor. Metaphor is the essence of poetry and it appears most strongly in the lyric. But metaphor is necessary to all thought. Thought cannot find its beginning points without it. Whenever we encounter metaphor it transports the mind to a new mode. The world is originally made by us through metaphors, and the poet continually remakes the world for us. A great poet never leaves language the same, and language is never the same for the reader of great poetry. We can no more steal the club of Hercules than we can steal a line of Shakespeare.

From the study of the philosophers we learn the nature and the power of the idea. The great discovery of Plato is the idea that there are ideas. The idea contains the form of the world. It is the unseen that provides access to the seen. There is always more before the mind than there is in it, but what is in the mind—the idea—is what allows us to have an object before the

---

79. Ibid.
80. Ibid.

mind. The idea is what guides *logos* or speech. Through speech we hold the idea in mind.

The idea provides a logic of genus and species. The genus gathers the specific senses of things of a given type under it. The finding of the similar in dissimilars that we achieve in the metaphor is extended into the idea as genus. Once in possession of the genus we can grasp the world as a single order of species, genera, and *infima species* that allows the mind to extend its power beyond that of the metaphorical power simply to combine things. Metaphor has a natural home in meter, but putting philosophy in meter does not make it poetry. As Aristotle says in the *Poetics*: "Homer and Empedocles, however, have really nothing in common apart from their metre; so that, if the one is to be called a poet, the other should be termed a physical philosopher rather than a poet."[81]

From the study of the orators we learn the nature and importance of topics (*topoi*) as the source of eloquence. Topics are those commonplaces stored up in memory, the cultural archetypes we all share. They are the communal sense of the world that we have as human beings, expressed in the master images that we find in myths and literature, such as the earth mother, the dark wood, the divine child, the hidden king, the magic journey, the celestial ladder, the demon, the divine light, the shadow, the fountain of youth. To speak well we draw forth, from this treasure-house of human memory, points that we wish to make so as to have others comprehend our thoughts. We remember by storing up specific images in our memory, giving us an inner writing. From this inner writing we can pass from one point to the next, producing coherence in our speech. From these master images, as they become present to us as themes in literature, we can draw forth more specific images or metaphors from which to speak.

From the study of the historians we learn the art of narration. The source of history is the epic. As mentioned earlier, the writing of history is the joining of the literary imagination with the scientific conception of facts. Histories give us a grasp of temporal order writ large. They show us how the institutions of the great city of the human race succeed each other and how events repeat themselves even while changing in their form. Our study of histories allows us to transcend the present—to think beyond the present. Histories teach us how to approach events in the world in terms of beginning, middle, and end, in the way that the Muses can sing of what was, is, and is to come. This sequence is the special teaching of Clio. From

---

81. Aristotle, *Poetics* 1447b.

Introduction

histories we learn the meaning and truth of Faulkner's observation, that: "The past is never dead. It's not even past."[82] Reading the canon of great books makes the past present and, since things repeat in history, it readies us for the future. The canon of great books is the great teacher of prudence, the wisdom required to live the human, examined life.

Harold Bloom, in his study of the Western canon, begins with an elegy for it. He says: "The Canon, once we view it as the relation of an individual reader and writer to what has been preserved out of what has been written, and forget the canon as a list of books for required study, will be seen as identical with the literary Art of Memory."[83] The citizen of the Republic of Letters, seated in a study, encompassed by books with desk, pen, and writing paper, prepared to read, write, study, and cite from the works that comprise the school of the ages, is an anachronism, a person chronologically out of place, a holdover from the sixteenth, seventeenth, eighteenth, and nineteenth centuries. In the technological society all that is present is the illuminated screen of Plato's cave, with thought equated with information and joined to waves of opinion, one thing as accessible as another.

The Republic of Letters, its term emerging, in Latin, as *respublica litteraria* in the early fifteenth century, and later taken up by Jean Bodin, Erasmus, and Voltaire, is nowhere to be found. As Pierre Bayle defined it in his *Dictionnaire historique et critique*, it was a state of the mind governed by the authority of truth and reason. In the *Encyclopedia* of Diderot and d'Alembert, it was a society of learned people involved in rational investigation of all fields of knowledge. The Republic of Letters was a free association of scholars and investigators throughout Europe and America, an ideal tied to no particular borders or national interests. Its cosmopolitanism was the basis of modernity. But its sense of learning and modernity has been replaced by technology, which brings everything to its own level, including thought. The art of memory that is an art of coherence of mind is replaced by the amassing of information, the simple method of the storehouse.

The reading of literature and the scientific pursuit of knowledge for its own sake is largely unknown. Human education is perceived, not as the transmission of culture from one generation to another, but as an activity governed by the production of outcomes and their constant assessment. The classroom is not a sanctuary in which the mind is allowed to move freely, relieved of the need to justify the *eudaimonia* of contemplation. The

---

82. Faulkner, *Requiem for a Nun*, act 1, scene 3.
83. Bloom, *Western Canon*, 17.

The Philosophy of Literature

afflatus that seized Hegel in the Jena lecture rooms (see chapter 4, below) is inconceivable in today's administrated programs of instruction, with their emphasis on group projects, volunteerism, and the reduction of ideas to what is immediately understandable and agreeable. Contemporary teaching and learning demands the genius of mediocrity. Eccentricity is administratively precluded.

In the middle of the Wasteland that is this state of affairs is still the spark of the intellect of which Plato speaks as the means of the transmission of his doctrine. Ideas, whether Platonic, Neo-Platonic, Kantian, or Hegelian remain there to be found in the mind by those who may chance upon them. Once ideas are experienced in the great works of philosophy or in the great works of literature, the bibles of Homer, Dante, Shakespeare, and Goethe and all that surrounds them in the great canon, they cannot be forgotten. They are the eternal objects of the human self in its natural inclination to follow the Delphic instruction. The desire that all human beings have to know cannot be put aside by the insistence on pragmatic goals. The great books make the ideas they contain open to everyone. They are not exclusive. To reduce their significance to political standpoints is to miss their transcendence of the ages in which they appear. There are those who know, those who can come to know, and there are those who do not know.

The mind that does not know is not in a state of ignorance, for ignorance is the necessary, noble condition of wonder that generates curiosity. The mind that does not know is that which thinks only in political terms and thus is unable to seek the True, having already found it in the thought of the terrestrial city. The divine city of ideas remains unknown to it. The natural desire to know has been brought under control. For those who choose not to search out the divinity of the great ideas, they can only be offered the wishes of Oswald Spengler, as he expressed them in his study *The Decline of the West*, that if "those of the new generation devote themselves to technics instead of lyrics, the navy instead of painting, politics instead of epistemics, so they do, it is what I wish, and one cannot wish them better."[84]

Spengler described what was to come with the greatest accuracy. What was to come is now. It is in this technical climate that those who wish to read and to write must do so. In so doing we may keep in mind the words of Leonardo Bruni: "the intellect that aspires to the best must be in this way doubly educated [in literary skill and scientific knowledge], and it is for the sake of acquiring these two knowledges that we mass up our reading; yet we

---

84. Spengler, *Untergang des Abendlandes*, 56. My translation.

Introduction

must also take stock of the time at our disposal, devoting ourselves only to the most important and the most useful subjects, and not waste time with the obscure and profitless."[85] Better advice for the study of philosophy and literature is not to be found.

In taking this advice the solitary reader in a world that has given up the study of books can take consolation in the most ancient wisdom concerning the immortality of time: "What has been is what will be, and what has been done is what will be done; there is nothing new under the sun. Is there a thing of which it is said, 'See, this is new'? It has already been in the ages before us. The people of long ago are not remembered, nor will there be any remembrance of people yet to come by those who come after them" (Eccl 1:9–11). The ethics of the immortality of time suggests that what is worth doing between our remembered beginning and our anticipated end is the cultivation of the spirit that is offered through enrollment in the school of the ages that is begun in the school of the mythological poets and is taken up by the School of Athens and later by the Latins. Human education is finally nothing more than memory, the art inherent in all arts, the art of combining opposites and of seeing beyond the present.

---

85. Bruni, "Study of Literature," 123.

1

The Ethics of Immortality of Borges's *El inmortal*

Borges and Vico

Some writers, both literary and philosophical, presume their readers to be as learned as they are themselves. Borges and Vico share this presumption. With a natural ease, Vico can refer to such figures as Diodorus Siculus, Censorinus, Livius Andronicus, and Lactantius Firmianus as though the reader had them well in mind. With the same ease, Borges can refer to the outskirts of Bulaq prison in Samarkand, Bikaner, and Kolzvar as though they could be readily recognized. In both Borges and Vico, such learned references are mixed with images of great vivacity, such as Vico's portrait of Jove as the embodiment of thunder—Jupiter Tonans—or Borges's City of the Immortals. They confront us as readers with a style we may call poetic learning. They are *philologoi* who transport us from the present into the immense sublimity of the past.

We enter the great time of origin and of the past—the time outside of the time of the ongoing present—the time from which everything comes. Reading Borges and Vico takes us out of ourselves so that we see the past as present. We see how the past is always with us. But for the mind that has never read a Borges or a Vico, the past is not simply past; the past never really was. It is not surprising, then, that Borges, in his little masterpiece *El inmortal*, involves his reader in Vico's masterpiece, the *Scienza nuova*. Both

The Philosophy of Literature

Borges and Vico allow us to confront the seeming incomprehensibility of history; through them we glimpse the eternal in the temporal. For Borges this confrontation takes the form of questions concerning the nature of immortality and infinity. For Vico it takes the form of the presence of providence in the guise of his *storia ideal eterna* (ideal eternal history)—the three ages of gods, heroes, and humans that the nations undergo in their births, rises, and falls.

Borges and Vico face history as the great theater of memory that is the *Theatrum mundi*, on whose stage we as individuals appear briefly and then are gone—at most, perhaps, to leave a mark on collective memory. This mark can be preserved in words. Borges and Vico know the truth that all books are about other books. Through books our thoughts may remain in memory. The writings of Borges and Vico are recourses of other writings, other times.

The style of Borges and Vico is opposite to the principle of Ockham's razor—not to multiply assertions or entities. Their principle, instead, is the magnet—to draw into any work all that the mind can attract. The whole is Vico's flower of wisdom. Vico's *New Science* is a complete speech in which all that can be said of the nature of humanity is said. For Borges, the whole that is wisdom is ideally expressed in a fiction of a few pages. Such a fiction is a microcosm, and as such, a complete thought.

The Immortal has a central place in Borges's writings and is connected to several of his essays on infinity and the circularity of time. In his Norton lectures at Harvard, which appeared as the little volume *This Craft of Verse*, Borges, reflecting on how he conceived his fictions, gives *The Immortal* as an example. He says: "I thought of a quite good plot; then I wrote the story *El Inmortal*. The idea behind that story—and the idea might come as a surprise to any of you who have read the story—is that if a man were immortal, then in the long run (and the run *would* be long, of course), he would have said all things, written all things."

Borges continues: "I took as my example Homer; I thought of him (if indeed he existed) as having written his *Iliad*. Then Homer would go on living, and he would change as the generations of men have changed. Eventually, of course, he would forget his Greek, and in due time he would forget he had been Homer." Borges concludes: "This idea of Homer forgetting that he was Homer is hidden under many structures I wove around the book."[1]

---

1. Borges, *Craft of Verse*, 112–13.

The Ethics of Immortality of Borges's *El inmortal*

Homer would forget his Greek, as humanity itself has largely forgotten Homeric Greek. Yet Homer is the ideal figure for this story because he represents the origin of Western literature that is preserved in the Western canon. With Homer the Western literary imagination begins. To preserve the memory of Homer requires that we preserve the memory that is the Western canon. And to understand the writings of Borges and Vico we must preserve this memory, because it is from the contents of it that they, and all others like them, write.

Borges's *ficción* of the immortality of Homer is not an academic commentary on Vico's conception of the circularity of history, or Vico's "discovery of the true Homer." It offers us a different way than that of Benedetto Croce's *La filosofia di Giambattista Vico* or Isaiah Berlin's *Vico and Herder* and the range of philosophical studies that succeed them in Italian, English, French, German, and Spanish. In Borges's literary guise, Vico appears anew. We find Vico, to use his own terms, as a "poetic character" or "imaginative universal" (*universale fantastico*). We find him as a figure of the fantastic imagination, of Borges's fantastic imagination.

Borges's fiction of *The Immortal* is an example of the philosophy of literature conceived in the sense of philosophy *as* literature—as an example of literary philosophy. On this conception literature is understood in the broadest sense, as the power of the word to embody thought. The great works of philosophy, such as those of Plato or Hegel, are seen as intellectual narratives, the self in dialogue with itself. The great works of literature, such as those of Dante or Goethe, are inherently narratives of the intellect as well as of the imagination. Great works of philosophy and great works of literature arise from the same impetus and point in the same direction—the attempt to grasp what is absolute. Both philosophy and literature, in the ultimate sense, are attempts to take language beyond itself and to allow the mind to approach the really real. Philosophy and literature seen in this way are two sides of a coin. Neither can be fully separated from the other. The philosopher becomes a literary thinker and the litterateur becomes a lover of wisdom. They are both parts of a single process of the human spirit.

The Immortal may be described as an instance of literary philosophy because in it, image and idea are bound together so as to take the reader to a glimpse of the absolute through the interconnection of memory, time, and mortality. The unseen appears in the seen, yet remains in essence unseen. A fiction, as we encounter it at the pen of Borges, is a verbal emblem in which a large and complex meaning is condensed into a particular circle of thought. A fiction is not a novelty. It brings to mind elements of other works in the way that an emblem is composed of elements derived from other emblems.

Borges says: "It is a laborious madness and an impoverishing one, the madness of composing vast books—setting out in five hundred pages an idea that can be perfectly related orally in five minutes. The better way to go about it is to pretend that those books already exist, and offer a summary, a commentary on them."[2] He says he takes this procedure of writing from other writings—from Carlyle's *Sorter Resartus* and Butler's *The Fair Haven*. He carries this procedure even further in some cases, by writing about imaginary books. Fiction becomes tautological—fiction about fiction.

At another place, commenting on his fictions, Borges says: "I have tried (I am not sure how successfully) to write plain tales. I dare not say they are simple; there is not a simple page, a simple word on earth—for all pages, all words, predicate the universe, whose most notorious attribute is its complexity." All words are about other words, just as all works are about other works. Borges says, further: "But I do wish to make clear that I am not, nor have I ever been, what used to be called a fabulist or spinner of parables, what these days is called an *auteur engagé*. I do not aspire to be Æsop. My tales, like those of the *Thousand and One Nights*, are intended not to persuade readers, but to entertain and touch them. This intention does not mean that I shut myself, as Solomon's image would have it, into an ivory tower."

Fictions are not fantasies or parables, that is, they are not retreats from the world or moral allegories. They allow the reader to think thoughts which, if expressed in purely discursive terms, would lose the complexities of their truth. What is truly simple is always in fact complex. As Borges continues: "Each language is a tradition, each word a shared symbol; the changes that an innovator may make are trifling—we should remember the dazzling but often unreadable work of a Mallarmé or a Joyce."[3]

All bad philosophy is sincere. The opposite of sincerity, in this regard, is not insincerity but irony. Irony is the trope that governs both philosophy and fictions. Discovered by Socrates as the instrument of his thought, irony inhabits all true philosophy. Irony affords the mind distance from the matter in hand, non-attachment. It is this distance that we find in ourselves as philosophers and as readers of a fiction. The mind can hold something

---

2. Borges, "Foreword (1944)," in *Fictions*, 67.
3. Borges, "Foreword," in *Fictions*, 345–46.

before it, knowing that it can never fully know (and certainly not literally know) what is before it. There is always more before the mind than what it can perceive and what it can hold in thought. Philosophical thought is in principle ironic. Truth is always partial. What is thought and what is not thought, its opposite, both have a claim to truth. The True, then, is the whole. The sense of the whole is what is captured in the fiction as well as in the philosophical narrative.

The Fiction

Much of Vico's *New Science* has the character of a philosophical fiction, especially his retelling of the biblical flood and the race of giants that follow from it that is the basis of his poetic metaphysics upon which all of the new science is based. Borges's attachments to the importance of memory and fictive grasp of ideas, as well as Joyce's, have a natural sympathy with Vico's approach to thought and language that unites philosophy and philology by paying close attention to the etymology of words.

In the opening lines of *The Immortal*, the rare-book dealer Joseph Cartaphilus, who sells the volumes of Pope's *Iliad* to the Princess de Lucinge, in London, is also Vico, who, like Cartaphilus, has a friendly love of paper (Italian: *carta* = paper; Greek: *philos* = friendly, Latinized to *philus*). The bookseller is described as "an emaciated, grimy man with gray eyes and gray beard and singularly vague features [*un hombre consumido y terroso, de ojos grises y barba gris, de rasgos singularmente vagos*]."[4] Vico's early biographer, Nicola Solla, describes Vico as being "of medium height, his body tended to be adust [*adusto*], aquiline nose, and lively penetrating eyes."[5] Vico was a gaunt, adust, and melancholic figure, all skin and bones, derisively called (by his *gran tormentatore*, Nicola Capasso), "maestro Tisicuzzo," an antique slur meaning tubercular (*tisico*).

Vico's father was a bookseller in Naples; his bookshop was in San Biagio dei Librai (*libraio*, bookseller, bookshop), one of the system of streets commonly called *Spaccanapoli* because they split the ancient center of Naples in two. Vico was born and raised in the single room in which his family lived, above his father's shop. In 1726, the year following the publication of the first edition of his *New Science*, Vico served as appraiser of the library of Giuseppe Valletta, the best in Naples. In preparing the *New*

---

4. Borges, *Immortal*, 183.
5. Verene, *New Art of Autobiography*, 28–29.

The Philosophy of Literature

Science, Vico said: "I entombed myself completely in the silence of a great library rich in all the various works of human thought, where I meditated on the most ancient authors of all nations from whom after more than a thousand years modern writers take their beginnings."[6] The *New Science* throughout is built upon citations to other works. Vico is a lover of books, of writings, of what appears on paper.

The manuscript that is bound into the last volume of Pope's *Iliad* that the Princess buys is the text of *The Immortal* that is declared to be written in English but that "teems" with Latinisms. Borges's Spanish rendering of it also teems with Latinisms. Vico's *Scienza nuova* is traditionally regarded as written in a Latinized style, thought to be so because Vico wrote his prior works in Latin and from the fact that Vico prided himself as having mastered Latin equally with his own language. Vico's oration on education *De nostri temporis studiorum ratione*, is composed in an exceptional Latin style.

Once he has passed on the manuscript hidden in the *Iliad*, Cartaphilus, the double of Vico, dies on his way back to his birthplace, Smyrna, as Borges relates. Smyrna is in western Turkey, south of the ancient location of Troy. Borges says Cartaphilus "expressed himself with untutored and uncorrected fluency in several languages."[7] This mixture of languages may indicate a mixture of previous identities, indicating that he may be one of the immortals, having lived many lives. Now, having passed on the manuscript regarding the immortals, Cartaphilus can finally achieve mortality and be returned to his humanity. He is buried on the Greek island of Ios in the south central Cyclades, in the Aegean Sea.

If we accept the opinion of Pindar, who holds that Homer's birthplace was Smyrna, Cartaphilus may also be Homer. That Cartaphilus speaks in various languages and dialects may reflect the fact that, according to Vico, Homer's poems combine dialects of various Greek peoples, leading to the view that this is why so many Greek cities claim to be his birthplace. Homer's works are not transmitted in any one dialect but in as many Greek dialects as there are cities that claim to be his birthplace.[8]

---

6. Vico, *Vici Vindiciae*, 134.

7. Borges, *Immortal*, in *Fictions*, 183. Quotations from *Immortal* hereinafter are cited above by the section numbers in Borges's text.

8. On the birthplace of Homer, see *Lives of Homer* 1.1. On Pindar's view (fr. 279), see "Homer," in *Oxford Classical Dictionary*, 524.

The Ethics of Immortality of Borges's *El inmortal*

The manuscript describes an odyssey subsequent to that of Odysseus, of a warrior in the service of the emperor Diocletian in the revolt in Egypt in AD 296, which was suppressed by Diocletian in person at Alexandria the following year. The warrior-narrator says he "had fought (with no glory) in the recent Egyptian wars and was tribune of a legion quartered in Berenice, on the banks of the Red Sea" (1). Although quartered in Berenice, a city founded by Ptolemy, he says his "travails began in a garden in hundred-gated Thebes." This is the Egyptian Thebes, formerly capital of Egypt, on the left bank of the Nile. The reference to the hundred-gated Thebes is to its description in the ninth book of the *Iliad*. Diocletian was known not only for his conquests but for his attachment to the old Roman religion, traditions, and discipline.

The narrator of the text is confronted by an exhausted rider, whose birthplace is beyond the Ganges, and who is in search of "the secret river that purifies men of death" (1). He dies before dawn, but not before relating that "on the far shore of that river lay the City of the Immortals" (1). The narrator decides to go in search of that city. He encounters great difficulties, can find no water, and his men desert him. He is obsessed with the image of the City. He dreams of an "orderly labyrinth at whose center lay a well." But he dreams: "I knew I would die before I reached it" (1). Then he wakes from this nightmare to find himself before the City of the Immortals, surrounded by a group of Troglodytes, who survive by devouring serpents. We then learn his full identity: "Marcus Flaminius Rufus, military tribune of one of the legions of Rome" (2). Flaminius Rufus drinks from the river the rider had sought. He says: "I plunged my bloodied face into the dark water and lapped it like an animal" (2).

He enters the City of the Immortals to find that, instead of being a wondrous labyrinth of divine design, it is a deconstructed architecture such that "the width and height of the treads on the staircases were not constant." He says the architecture had no purpose. "There were corridors that led nowhere, unreachably high windows, grandly dramatic doors that opened onto monklike cells or empty shafts, incredible upside-down staircases with upside-down treads and balustrades." He decides that the "*gods that built this place were mad.*" It "*pollutes the past and the future and somehow compromises the stars. So long as the City endures, no one in the world can ever be happy or courageous*" (2). When he emerges he swears to put this experience out of his memory.

The Philosophy of Literature

Who is Marcus Flaminius Rufus? Why must he erase so far as possible any memory of this city? Unlike Odysseus he is not royal, but his name is patrician. Marcus is a common Roman *praenomen*—the name, for example, of Cicero's son. Flaminius is a patrician surname from the Roman gens Quinctius. Rufus has noble associations—Rufus of Ephesus, the noted physician who had a knowledge of Egypt, and Quintus Curtius Rufus, who published a large history of Alexander the Great. He had expected the city to be a great work of the gods, an ideal city made actual and eternal, but it is a nightmare of deconstruction and disorder. The hope of something eternal being a perfection—that can be set off against the imperfection of temporal existence—is dashed. What is immortal, eternal, is space and time gone mad. We are better off not to know of it.

Flaminius Rufus is left with the companionship of a single Troglodyte, who attaches himself to him and follows him in the manner of a faithful dog or horse. He says: "The Troglodyte's lowly birth and condition recalled to my memory of the image of Argos, the moribund old dog of the *Odyssey*, so I gave him the name Argos, and tried to teach it to him" (3). He fails time and time again to get the Troglodyte to respond to the name. He reflects "that it is generally believed among the Ethiopians that monkeys deliberately do not speak, so that they will not be forced to work; I attributed Argos' silence to distrust or fear" (3). He realizes that the Troglodyte and he likely live in separate universes; that of the Troglodyte is one of swift impressions devoid of memory and thus without objects that populate the human world. Then in desperation, in a rainstorm in the frigid desert night, Flaminius Rufus cries out: "*Argos!*" (3).

Suddenly, in answer, "Argos stammered out these words: *Argos, Ulysses' dog*. And then, without looking at me, *This dog lying on the dungheap*" (3). This is the dog that appears in the seventeenth book of the *Odyssey*, when Odysseus returns to Ithaca, and that is living on top of "piles of dung from mules and cattle." Now very old, Argos recognizes his returned master by wagging his tail and dropping his ears instead of pricking his ears, as he did at strangers. Argos dies as soon as he recognizes Odysseus. Then Odysseus, in the guise of a beggar, follows Eumaeus, the local swineherd, into his own royal house to confront the suitors.

In the odyssey of Marcus Flaminius Rufus, Argos the Troglodyte is Homer. He says: "I asked Argos how much of the *Odyssey* he knew. He found using Greek difficult; I had to repeat the question. *Very little*, he replied. *Less than the meagerest rhapsode. It has been eleven hundred years*

The Ethics of Immortality of Borges's *El inmortal*

since I wrote it" (3). Homer explains that the Troglodytes were the immortals. The city had existed as a marvel, but the Immortals had destroyed this version about nine hundred years ago and on the same spot they had built the incoherent city as a temple to the irrational gods that rule the world and who do not resemble men. Then the Immortals abandoned this city and went off to dwell in caves and exist only as self-absorbed beings, scarcely perceiving the physical world.

Homer, after composing his poems, had gone in search of the Immortals and lived for a century in the City of the Immortals. When it was destroyed it was Homer who counseled the incoherent city be built as its replacement. We are told: "We should not be surprised by that—it is rumored that after singing of the War of Ilion, he sang of the war between the frogs and rats. He was like a god who created first the Cosmos, and then Chaos" (4).

In the *Homeric Apocrypha*, in the "Battle of the Frogs and the Rats" the gods, at the advice of Athena, allow the meaningless event to take place. Athena says: "gods, let's forget aiding these creatures, in case one of you gets wounded by a sharp missile: they are close fighters, even if a god should come against them. Let's all just enjoy watching the battle from heaven. So she spoke, and the other gods went along with her advice."[9] The war between these two species is without meaning. It is chaotic activity that simply ends, as the poem describes, when the day itself ends.

The manuscript states: "There is nothing very remarkable about being immortal; with the exception of mankind, all creatures are immortal, for they know nothing of death. What is divine, terrible and incomprehensible is *to know* oneself immortal" (4). Mortality is the necessary condition of the desire for virtue, for the best life. The Immortal lives all lives and need not prefer one over the other. "No one is someone; a single immortal man is all men" (4). Mortality is the condition that generates the drive to create meaning, to make literature. "Homer composed the *Odyssey*; given infinite time, with infinite circumstances and changes, it is impossible that the *Odyssey* should *not* be composed at least once" (4). To be all things is the same as to be not. For to be is to be something particular, individual, that cannot be completely duplicated and that can pass out of existence.

In the life of mortals everything is contingent. "Among the Immortals, on the other hand, every act (every thought) is the echo of others that preceded it in the past, with no visible beginning, and the faithful presage

---

9. *Homeric Apocrypha* 193–97.

of others that will repeat it in the future, *ad vertiginem*" (4). The existence of the Immortal is a turning around on itself without end. There is no past, present, and future. One thing is always counterbalanced by another. The Immortals are prevented from having any sense of pity, for any wrong will eventually be balanced by a right and the reverse. It is comparable to betting in games of chance: winnings and losings tend to equal out over time.

Flaminius Rufus and Homer separate, and the manuscript relates how this Roman Ulysses wandered through "new realms" and "new empires," fighting in the battle of Stamford Bridge in 1066 in the ranks of Harold II and wandering through the centuries in the cultures of Europe and the East (5). He recorded the seven voyages of Sindbad and taught astrology in Bikaner in northwest India and in Bohemia in central Europe. He subscribed to the six volumes of Pope's *Iliad* in Aberdeen in 1714, just prior to its publication, which began in 1715, as noted earlier. He says: "In 1729 or thereabouts, I discussed the origin of that poem with a professor of rhetoric whose name, I believe, was Giambattista; his arguments struck me as irrefutable" (5). On his way to Bombay in 1921 Flaminius Rufus drinks from a spring on the Eritrean coast and while so doing scratches the back of his hand on a thorn. A drop of blood appears, and he realizes he is once more mortal.

The True Homer

In the last several paragraphs of the manuscript, the tale told in the first person by Marcus Flaminius Rufus breaks off. These paragraphs contain a reflection on the credibility of the tale by Cartaphilus, who claims that what is related does not pass beyond the bounds of truth but in some details he detects "a certain falseness." He says it is "a way of writing that I learned from poets; it is a procedure that infects everything with falseness" (5). This claim echoes that in the *Ars poetica* of Horace, in which he acknowledges that poets make things up but also advises that poetry should not be inconsistent. The poet naturally fills in what is lost to memory. Cartaphilus is speaking for Borges himself in saying: "it does not matter that I may be judged a fantast [*fantástico*]" (5).

The reason for the intermingling of truth and falseness is that the memories of two figures are intermingled—that of Flaminius Rufus and of Homer. This intermingling is characteristic of the poet inspired by the Muses, the daughters of Memory who sing both true and false songs, but

The Ethics of Immortality of Borges's *El inmortal*

can sing true songs when they will. The Roman is both a warrior like Ulysses and a man of letters like Homer because on several occasions, especially when he first drinks the water of the river of the Immortals, he speaks the words of Homer that appear at the end of the famous catalogue of ships of the *Iliad*, of the "clan that drank the Aesepus' dark waters." The tale has thus been "composed by a man of letters desirous (like the author of the catalog of ships) of wielding splendid words." To this line is appended the footnote: "Ernesto Sabato suggests that the 'Giambattista' who discussed the origins of the *Iliad* with the rare book dealer Cartaphilus is Giambattista Vico, the Italian who defended the argument that Homer is a symbolic character, like Pluto or Achilles" (5).

Finally, both Flaminius Rufus and Cartaphilus assert that now, at the end of their lives, they have lost all images supplied by memory and all that remains are words. The Roman Ulysses says: "As the end approaches, there are no longer any images from memory—there are only words" (5). The "me" of memory—with its storehouse of images formed as an individual—is gone. Flaminius Rufus says: "I have been Homer, soon like Ulysses, I shall be Nobody [*outis*]; soon, I shall be all men—I shall be dead" (5). The manuscript ends with these words: "*As the end approaches*, wrote Cartaphilus, *there are no longer any images from memory—there are only words*. Words, words, words taken out of place and mutilated, words from other men—those were the alms left him by the hours and the centuries" (5). The immortal becomes a fiction without unique identity. Flaminius Rufus becomes a fantast telling the story of his life—the story made up of the words of other fictions. Thought is now just the manipulation of words in a present.

What is Vico's account of Homer, the arguments of which seem irrefutable? In the third book of the *New Science*, Vico engages in a digression addressed to the "Discovery of the True Homer." It confirms the claim of the abovementioned footnote, that Vico regards Homer as a "symbolic character [*personaje simbólico*]." Vico says: "Homer was an idea or a heroic character of Grecian men [*un carattere eroico d'uomini greci*] insofar as they told their histories in song."[10] Vico takes a position between the views that Homer did not exist and that Homer is an abstract symbol. Instead, Vico regards Homer as actual but not in the sense of a given individual. Homer is a collective name for those ancient Greeks who narrated their histories in song. Homer, then, is a generic name of the imagination, or what Vico calls

---

10. Vico, *New Science*, par. 873.

a "poetic character" or "imaginative universal" (*universale fantastico*), the logic of which is at the basis of all fables.

The two examples the footnote gives of such characters—Pluto and Achilles—are not the standard combination that Vico gives. His two constant examples of heroic characters are Achilles and Ulysses, the heroes of the two Homeric poems. All gods and heroes are poetic characters. Pluto, one of the children of Kronos, is not a hero but a god with the Roman name Dis. He is likely included here because of his association with the underworld, and Vico has several passages interpreting Pluto escorting Proserpine into the underworld.[11] Vico identifies Proserpine with Ceres, the goddess of grain, a symbol of ancient wealth, and with the fable of Aeneas the Trojan-Roman Ulysses and the golden bough.

Vico says that the discovery that the first Gentile peoples were theological poets who spoke in poetic characters, and thus expressed the origin myths upon which all nations are founded, is "the master key of this Science."[12] These first humans could not form abstract class terms or "intelligible universals" (*universali intelligibili*) as formulated in Aristotle's *Organon*. They formed the primordial experience of thunder as Jove by onomatopoeia. The thunderous interjections of Jove gave birth to one produced by the human voice: "*pa*" which was then doubled as "*pape!*"[13] Prior to formulating the first name, "Jove," the first humans or protohumans, like the Troglodyte Argos, experienced the world as a series of fleeting impressions without the impressions coming together as objects. Each instance of thunder was a unique perception. The sudden finding of the meaning of the whole series in one of these perceptions produces Jove as the first named object.

Once in possession of the power of the name, everything can be named and all flora and fauna become gods. Vico says: "The first founders of humanity applied themselves to a sensory topics [*topica sensibile*], by which they brought together those properties or qualities or relations of individuals and species which were, so to speak, concrete, and from these formed their poetic genera."[14] These topics are formed not by reflection or intellection but by imagination (*fantasia*) and memory. Vico says in his discussion of Homer that "memory is the same as imagination [*la memoria è la stessa*

---

11. Ibid., pars. 714, 716, and 721.
12. Ibid., par. 34.
13. Ibid., par. 448.
14. Ibid., par. 495.

che la fantasia]."¹⁵ The first humans, like children, have strong memories and thus strong imaginations; they think in poetic characters. Vico says: "'Character' means idea, form, model; and certainly poetic characters came before those of articulate sounds [that is, before alphabetic characters]."¹⁶

In Vico's "ideal eternal history" of three ages through which any nation develops—the ages of gods, heroes, and humans—poetic characters or universals are the thought-form of the ages of gods and heroes, and intelligible class-concepts or universals are the form of the human age. Once a nation develops to its heroic age it can employ heroes as poetic characters that embody virtues which direct behavior. The human mind at this age is unable to form moral abstractions such as courage or wisdom (*prudentia, phronesis*). It forms these as the heroic characters of Achilles and Ulysses.

All warriors who are courageous are perceived as Achilles. All warriors who are prudent and clever are Ulysses. These individuals are not *like* Achilles or Ulysses. They literally *are* them, and in addition Achilles is Achilles and Ulysses is Ulysses. That Achilles and Ulysses are one and many at the same time in the same sense is a meaning that can be reached only by the power of *fantasia*, not by rational reflection. Achilles and Ulysses can be univocally (literally) predicated of individuals in the same way that the rational mind can literally predicate the virtues of courage and prudence as properties of a class of individuals. The imaginative universal is phenomenologically presupposed by the intelligible universal (*universale intelligibile*).

The reflective or rational mind can have access to the logic of *fantasia* only through fictions. Once the world of mythical thinking is left, myth proper can never be made again. Lyric can capture only one aspect of the myth—the power of the immediate image. The lyric must be bonded with the dramatic and the epic to attain the fiction, because myth is more than immediate images. Myths, whether primal or societal, structure the world. Like the poetic characters upon which they are based, myths are a world of proto-thought accessible to an extent by the imagination, but whose inner form is not accessible to reason.

Vico says: "Aristotle in his *Poetics* says that only Homer knew how to invent poetic falsehoods. For his poetic characters, which are incomparable for the sublime appropriateness which Homer admires in them,

---

15. Ibid., par. 819.
16. Ibid., par. 429.

were imaginative universals."[17] As cited above in the introduction, Aristotle says: "Homer more than any other has taught the others [poets] the art of framing lies in the right way. I mean the use of paralogism. Whenever, if one thing is or happens, another is or happens, men's notion is that if the latter is, so is the former—but that is a false conclusion."[18] Vico points out, rightly, that Horace in *Ars poetica* advises poets above all to imitate Homer's creation of characters.[19] Paralogism is incorrect reasoning and has a connection to legend (Greek *para-logos*, against speech or reason; legend, akin to *legein*, to collect, gather, speak; *logos*).

A fiction is always a doubling-up. Two things can always be associated such that the presence of one seems to justify the presence of the other. As in an imaginative universal, Cartaphilus can be Vico and yet be Cartaphilus. Flaminius Rufus can be Homer and yet be the Roman tribune attracted to the use of letters. The imagination can tolerate what reason cannot. Yet it is in the imagination that original connections are made that supply the beginnings for the rational sense of *logos*. In the fiction we can think the unthinkable.

The epigraph Borges affixes to *The Immortal* is from Bacon's essay "Of Vicissitude of Things": "Solomon saith: *There is no new thing upon the earth*. So that as Plato had an imagination, *that all knowledge was but remembrance*; so Solomon giveth his sentence, *that all novelty is but oblivion*."[20]

A source for Bacon's sense of vicissitude is Machiavelli's observation in the *Discourses*: "that things are forgotten." Machiavelli says: "To those philosophers who have held that the world is eternal, I believe it can be replied that, if such antiquity is correct, it is reasonable that there should be a record of more than five thousand years, except that such records of the past are blotted out by various causes, part of which come from men, part from Heaven."[21] Only what repeats itself in some way is remembered; what does not at some point is forgotten. Eternity depends upon repetition of events.

In the *Phaedo* Socrates says to Cebes that "coming to life again in truth exists, the living come to be from the dead, and the souls of the dead exist." Cebes replies that "for us learning is no other than recollection. According

---

17. Ibid., par. 809.
18. Aristotle, *Poetics* 1460a.
19. Vico, *New Science*, par. 806.
20. Bacon, "Of Vicissitude of Things," in *Major Works*, 451.
21. Machiavelli, *Discourses*, in *Chief Works*, 1:339-40.

The Ethics of Immortality of Borges's *El inmortal*

to this, we must at some previous time have learned what we now recollect. This is possible only if our soul existed somewhere before it took on this human shape. So according to this theory too, the soul is likely to be something immortal."[22] Knowledge, then, is dependent on what can be remembered and what can truly be remembered over time is what can repeat itself. What is purely novel disappears from memory because it is unconnected to the whole, which exists beyond time and which itself does not change.

At the beginning of Ecclesiastes, the author, who by tradition may be Solomon, puts forth the claim that all novelty is oblivion in the famous lines: "What has been is what will be, and what has been done is what will be done; there is nothing new under the sun." This claim of repetition is followed by: "Is there a thing of which it is said, 'See, this is new'? It has already been, in the ages before us." And then: "The people of long ago are not remembered, nor will there be any remembrance of people yet to come by those who came after them" (Eccl 9–11). The causes of oblivion are those that Machiavelli identifies: the acts of Heaven, natural disasters that destroy all records, and the acts of men's memory, which is affected as much by its powers of remembrance as by those of forgetting.

To endorse this view of vicissitude and also to offset it, we may add the maxim of the Florentine historian Francesco Guicciardini: "All that which has been in the past and is at present will be again in the future. But both the names and the appearances of things change, so that he who does not have a good eye will not recognize them. Nor will he know how to grasp a norm of conduct or make a judgment by means of observation."[23] Guicciardini's *buono occhio* is the key to prudence. The circularity of time is not simply the condition of change; it is the time of eternity. The eternal, the immortal is not a reality separate from the contingent world of change; it is the circularity and repetitiveness of that world itself.

The Circularity of Time and the Ethics of Immortality

In his non-fictions or essays Borges returns repeatedly to the subject of the circularity of time and the nature of immortality. In the "Doctrine of Cycles" (1936) he addresses the doctrine of the Eternal Return, which he finds in Nietzsche. Borges formulates it as: "*The number of all atoms that compose the world is immense but finite, and as such only capable of a finite*

---

22. Plato, *Phaedo* 72e.
23. Guicciardini, *Ricordi*, 131. My translation.

The Philosophy of Literature

(though also immense) number of permutations. In an infinite stretch of time, the number of possible permutations must be run through, and the universe has to repeat itself."[24] This doctrine of cycles is challenged, Borges says, by Georg Cantor's doctrine of transfinite numbers entailed in his arithmetic of the infinite and theory of sets of points.

On this conception all that there is can be considered finite, yet within this finitude we can conceive of an infinite progression that never wholly repeats itself. Such an infinite progression can be conceived in terms of temporal moments or sets of spatial points. Transfinite is either an index of the ordered set of all natural numbers or can be generated from these by purely algebraic means. Another way to see this principle is to regard a cardinal number of a mathematical aggregate as not finite.

Although Borges presents this conception of finite-infinite in terms of Cantor's sets, we may more easily view it in the broader epistemological terms of a logical function of the form $\varphi(x)$ where x is a series of variables constructed through its bond with a law of the series φ. The φ and the x are of different logical types yet have meaning only when taken together. The law of a particular series is meaningless when taken in itself and the variables in such a series have no meaning apart from the order that the law establishes in the series. Variables have no independent or intrinsic meaning as individuals. They are only individuals when serially ordered—when they are part of a progressively constructed whole. The $\varphi(x)$ is at any point finite, yet the series is infinite. At no point need it become a cycle or repeat itself.

In an essay of the same year, "A History of Eternity," Borges says: "as everyone knows—eternity is the model and archetype of time." He says: "For us, time is a jarring, urgent problem, perhaps the most vital problem of metaphysics."[25] Borges is at one with Hegel's claim that "the true infinite [*das wahrhafte Unendliche*] is the fundamental concept of philosophy [*der Grundbegriff der Philosophie*]."[26] All metaphysics depends upon the proper comprehension of the concept of infinity, which is the proper comprehension of time. Hegel distinguishes between the true infinite—the concept of an infinite progression that dialectically or functionally recapitulates itself (in the manner described above)—and the bad infinite (*die schlechte Unendlichkeit*)—an infinite series in which one thing simply comes after

---

24. Borges, "Doctrine of Cycles," in *Non-Fictions*, 115.
25. Borges, "A History of Eternity," in *Non-Fictions*, 123.
26. Hegel, *Die Wissenschaft der Logik*, Werke, 8:203. My translation.

The Ethics of Immortality of Borges's *El inmortal*

another and in which the finite and infinite are simple opposites, making the infinite conditioned by the finite. This is not an abstract problem, as Borges rightly holds, for time is the very condition of our human existence. In metaphysical terms, it is the problem of the finite and infinity or eternity. In anthropological terms, it is the problem of mortality and immortality.

In "When Fiction Lives in Fiction" (1939), Borges describes his first experience with infinity, which is his childhood notice of a Japanese scene painted on a large biscuit tin, in the corner of which reappears the same scene, in which appears the same scene, etc. Some years later he "discovered in one of Russell's works an analogous invention by Josiah Royce, who postulates a map of England drawn on a portion of the territory of England: this map—since it is exact—must contain a map of the map, which must contain a map of the map of the map, and so to infinity."[27] The source of this is most likely Royce's "Supplementary Essay" in *The World and the Individual*.[28] Borges sees, in this map and in the double portrait of Philip IV in Velázquez's *Las meninas*, the phenomenon of "the interpolation of a fiction within another fiction."[29] Since all books are about other books, as all artworks are about other artworks, a fiction is always a determinate moment either explicitly or implicitly in a "true infinity" of images.

In "Circular Time" (1941), Borges says: "I tend to return eternally to the Eternal Return." His purpose in these several pages is to define the three fundamental modes of the conception of circular time. The first is that attributed to Plato, which is the idea of a literal return to the past such that there will be, as Borges says Thomas Browne put it: "A revolution of a certain thousand years when all things should return to their former estate and he [Plato] be teaching again in his school as when he delivered this opinion."[30] The source for this conception of "Plato's year" is Augustine's *City of God*.[31] The second mode is that of Nietzsche, as discussed earlier. Borges finds this Nietzschean view stated in Hume's *Dialogues Concerning Natural Religion*, in which he considers the view that instead of supposing matter to be of an infinite number of particulars, as did Epicurus, we consider it finite. Hume writes: "This world, therefore, with all its events, even

---

27. Borges, "When Fiction Lives in Fiction," in *Non-Fictions*, 160.
28. Royce, *World and the Individual*, 504.
29. Borges, "Fiction," in *Non-Fictions*, 160.
30. Borges, "Circular Time," in *Non-Fictions*, 225.
31. Augustine, *City of God* 12.14.

the most minute, has before been produced and destroyed, and will again be produced and destroyed, without any bounds and limitations."[32]

Borges says: "I now arrive at the final mode of interpreting eternal repetitions, the least melodramatic and terrifying of the three, but the only one that is conceivable. I mean the concept of similar but not identical cycles. The infinite catalogue of authorities would be impossible to complete."[33] One of the authorities Borges cites is Vico, but he does not discuss Vico's conception of the life of nations as governed by *corso* and *ricorso*. He quotes Marcus Aurelius: "The lengthiest and briefest periods are equal. The present belongs to all; to die is to lose the present, which is the briefest of lapses. No one loses the past or the future, because no man can be deprived of what he does not have."[34] And Schopenhauer: "No man has lived in the past, and none will ever live in the future; the *present* alone is the form of all life."[35] That to be alive is simply to be in the present is the first consequence of this third mode of eternal repetitions. "The second is a negation of all novelty, following the author of Ecclesiastes [as quoted in the epigraph for *The Immortal*]."[36]

Vico's *corso*—his cycle of three ages of ideal eternal history—is followed by the *ricorso* of these ages. But the *ricorso* is not "Plato's year" of literal repetition, nor is it the eternal return of cycle after cycle in a finite universe. Vico's *ricorso* has the sense of a retrial in which he claims providence tries to teach its divine truth of a natural eternal republic a second time. The *ricorso* is a recollection of the *corso* and thus a repetition of it in different terms. Applied to Western history, the *corso* is the age of gods and heroes before Homer, whose poetry summarizes them and preserves them in the Greeks' common memory. The Homeric turning-point is followed by the heroic mind of Socratic reason that originates the distinctively human world of ideas and written laws that is continued by the Romans until the fall of ancient civilization.

The *ricorso* is a return to religion in the early medieval or "Dark Ages" of Europe. This period is followed by the High Middle Ages of chivalrous heroism and Scholastic thought that is summarized by Dante, the "Tuscan Homer," as Vico calls him. Dante is followed by the Renaissance Humanists,

32. Borges, "Circular Time," in *Non-Fictions*, 226. Quoted by Borges.
33. Ibid.
34. Ibid., 227.
35. Ibid.
36. Ibid.

The Ethics of Immortality of Borges's *El inmortal*

who revive the thought and culture of Athens and Rome, which then declines into the Cartesian world of ratiocination and a jurisprudence of laws as regulations rather than the embodiment of virtues.

Borges says we "all secretly share the same destiny—the only possible destiny—thus universal history is the history of a single man." Time and our fate of mortality now becomes tolerable. Borges further says that our allotted seventy years "becomes no more than an affirmation that the number of human perceptions, emotions, thoughts, and vicissitudes is limited and that before dying we will exhaust them all."[37] Vico's *corso* is childhood; his *ricorso* is adulthood. At any moment we are in the true infinity of the present. We have the assurance that at no time can we be imprisoned by external events, if we have this inner form of human memory. To extend Borges's point, we may add that this assurance presupposes an education of the soul—*paideia, Bildung*—which is the education of memory, for memory is the form of our humanity in the present. "Personal identity is known to reside in memory, and the annulment of that faculty is known to result in idiocy."[38] It is the teaching of the Muses, who can sing of what was, is, and is to come.

In "A New Refutation of Time" (1944–47), Borges says: "In the course of a life dedicated to belles-lettres and, occasionally, to the perplexities of metaphysics, I have glimpsed or foreseen a refutation of time, one in which I myself do not believe, but which tends to visit me at night and in the hours of weary twilight with the illusory force of a truism. This refutation is to be found in one form or another, in all my books."[39] To consider the question of the refutation of time Borges turns to Berkeley, the first figure of the modern version of philosophical idealism, Plato being such in the ancient world. Borges holds that idealism is perhaps the most ancient and most widely held doctrine in the history of philosophy.

Borges rightly puts aside the view that Berkeley's philosophy entails solipsism because "Berkeley affirmed the continuous existence of objects, inasmuch as when no individual perceives them, God does."[40] He also affirms Berkeley's ingenious refutation of the view that the mind can be material because the brain is simply an idea the mind has of itself. In Berkeley's

---

37. Ibid., 228.
38. Borges, "A History of Eternity," in *Non-Fictions*, 136.
39. Borges, "A New Refutation of Time," in *Non-Fictions*, 318.
40. Ibid., 320.

Three Dialogues, Philonous says: "The brain therefore you speak of, being a sensible thing, exists only in the mind."[41]

The idealist position as Borges describes it, moving from Berkeley to F. H. Bradley, is that succession is the condition of our perceptions and thoughts but succession does not apply to the Absolute as such. Temporal succession, then, is a property of our subjective mind but not of divine mind, which perceives all simultaneously as an eternal present. Yet Borges, having argued that the idealist denial of time as ultimately real is not logically refutable, concludes: "To deny temporal succession, to deny the self, to deny the astronomical universe, appear to be acts of desperation and are secret consolations." He says our destiny to be mortal is not terrifying because it is unreal; it is terrifying because it is irreversible. Nothing can prevent our death as a particular self, even if the really real of the Absolute is not in itself temporal, that is, if its being is not successive. Borges concludes: "Time is the substance of which I am made. Time is a river that sweeps me along, but I am the river; it is a tiger that mangles me, but I am the tiger; it is a fire that consumes me, but I am the fire. The world, unfortunately, is real; I, unfortunately, am Borges."[42]

We may connect this sense of the personal in relation to temporal succession with Borges's final remarks in his "A History of Eternity." There he relates a passage entitled "Feeling of Death," from his book *The Language of the Argentines*. It captures his personal theory of eternity. "Mine is an impoverished eternity, without God or even a co-proprietor, and entirely devoid of archetypes."[43] He describes walking, one evening, in an unfamiliar neighborhood. Suddenly he felt the simple scene he took in as if timeless. "I felt as the dead feel, I felt myself to be an abstract observer of the world: an indefinite fear imbued with knowledge that is the greatest clarity of metaphysics." The serenity of the night and of the scene produced a true sense of eternity. It was a sense of the unchanged, not of similarity or repetition of things but of something being absolutely the same.

Borges says: "When we can feel this oneness, time is a delusion which the indifference and inseparability of a moment from its apparent yesterday and from its apparent today suffice to disintegrate." He concludes: "Life is too impoverished not to be immortal. But we lack even the certainty of our own poverty, given that time, which is easily refutable by the senses, is not

---

41. Berkeley, *Three Dialogues*, 52.
42. Borges, "A New Refutation of Time," in *Non-Fictions*, 332.
43. Borges, "A History of Eternity," in *Non-Fictions*, 137.

The Ethics of Immortality of Borges's *El inmortal*

so easily refuted by the intellect, from whose essence the concept of succession appears inseparable."[44] Borges's "intimation of eternity" is a moment of metaphysical insight that overcomes the sense of *aporia* that Aristotle, in the beginning of the *Metaphysics*, describes as generating *thauma* (wonder), from which metaphysics originates.

Borges's final consideration of the problem of time is his lecture on "Immortality" (1978). Here he declares: "I don't want to continue being Jorge Luis Borges; I want to be someone else. I hope that my death will be total; I hope to die in body and soul." Borges says: "The most poignant text in all of philosophy, without trying to be so, is Plato's *Phaedon*."[45] This is the dialogue of Socrates's last day of life, in which Socrates discusses the question of the immortality of the soul with the two Pythagoreans, Simmias and Cebes, and which ends in the scene of his death. Borges marvels that on the last day of his life Socrates speaks of the inseparability of pleasure and pain as well as holding the soul to be separate from the body and that the soul, when freed from the body, can dedicate itself to thinking.

In this final lecture on the subject of immortality, Borges insists that he wishes to cease as Borges. After reviewing various philosophical views of the immortality of the soul, he concludes: "I would say that I believe in immortality, not in the personal but in the cosmic sense. We will keep on being immortal; beyond our physical death our memory will remain, and beyond our memory will remain our actions, our circumstances, our attitudes, all that marvelous part of universal history, although we won't know, and it is better that we won't know it."[46] Borges apparently sees his own immortality as that of those he includes within his own thoughts and writings. He will become one of the authors on whom other authors base their works. But Borges the actual man will be no more. Borges portrays himself as having reached a point at which he has been all he can be and he wants not to continue as a repetition of himself.

In his "Afterword," reflecting on the various fictions of *The Aleph*, Borges says the subject of "The Immortal" "is the effect that immortality would have on humankind," and that this text is an "outline for an ethics of immortality."[47] The metaphysics of infinity points to an ethics. Borges's considerations of infinity and immortality in his various non-fictions take

---

44. Ibid., 138.
45. Borges, "Immortality," in *Non-Fictions*, 484.
46. Ibid., 481.
47. Borges, "Afterword," in *Fictions*, 287.

us to the view that a concept of personal immortality is unnecessary for an ethics of humankind. For us to seek the best life it is not necessary for us to prove or believe in an afterlife in which the succession that characterizes temporal existence is overcome in an eternal present. The Kantian view that we require a sense of God as judge to be faced in an afterlife, in order to be moral in this life, is mistaken. The best life is its own reward. Borges quotes Plutarch: "Yesterday's man died in the man of today, today's man dies in the man of tomorrow."[48]

If we go to Plutarch's *Moralia*, we find that he adds: "Nobody remains one person, nor is one person; but we become many persons, even as matter is drawn about some one resemblance and common mould with imperceptible movement." We know this because we experience things differently at different times in our lives. Plutarch continues: "What, then, really is Being? It is that which is eternal, without beginning and without end, to which no length of time brings change. For time is something that is in motion, appearing in connexion with moving matter, ever flowing, retaining nothing, a receptacle, as it were, of birth and decay, whose familiar 'afterwards' and 'before,' 'shall be' and 'has been,' when they are uttered, are of themselves a confession of Not Being."[49]

Our Not Being is always at every moment in our Being. At death the successive sense of ourselves disappears and we are in time no more. Death gives us full access to Being. Whether this Being is that of our individual soul or a merger with the cosmic soul of *nous* remains an open question. It is evident by now that Borges's consideration of the interrelation of eternity and immortality, joined with the Vichian circularity of time, offers no intellectual solution to the problem of our mortality. We can confront this problem only existentially, not theoretically. It is an *aporia* not simply in thought but inscribed in the human condition itself. More we cannot say.

---

48. Borges, "A New Refutation of Time" in *Non-Fictions*, 331–32.
49. Plutarch, "The E at Delphi" 19.

2

The Metaphysics of *Finnegans Wake*

Facing Finnegans Wake

The reader of great books, at some point, perhaps by a "commodius vicus of recirculation," arrives at *Finnegans Wake*. This vicus may have run through *Dubliners*, especially its last chapter "The Dead," and through *A Portrait of the Artist as a Young Man*, the work of Joyce everybody reads, to *Ulysses*, the work that appears on every great books reading list but is often not fully read. Although *Ulysses* is a novel—the odyssey of Mr. Leopold Bloom during one day in Dublin (June 16, 1904)—*Finnegans Wake* is not. Of those readers who arrive at *Finnegans Wake*, only a few decide to cross its threshold and wander in its pages.

Those who enter *Finnegans Wake* begin to realize that, although full of stories, it is not itself a story. It is, in fact, Joyce's essay on man. It is not about individuals who develop in terms of a narration of their circumstances. *Finnegans Wake* lacks individuals; instead, its characters are human types. Its language is "basically English" (116.26).[1] But its language is its own, creating, in the tenth of its famous thunder words, the longest word in the English language—101 letters (424.20–22). The *Wake* is a world of

---

1. Throughout this chapter, citations to *Finnegans Wake* are given in the text, indicating page number and line to the 1939 first edition and its reprintings. Readers may also wish to be aware of the recent revised edition by Rose and O'Hanlon, showing a great number of small corrections. See bibliography, herein.

words, written in a language no one can speak. The events that take place in this world move toward no end. Like the world itself, everything and everybody is constantly repeated. The *Wake*, then, is "the hoax that joke bilked" (511.34), whose author is "Jeems Jokes," as Joyce signed his letter to his benefactor Harriet Shaw Weaver, which contained a key to a draft of the first lines of his work.[2]

Finnegans Wake is an extended joke made up of a countless number of individual jokes, done as puns. It is the longest joke in the English language or any other language. Jokes are a key to our humanity because, as Aristotle says, the human being is the "only animal that laughs."[3] Nora Joyce once reported that when Joyce was working, late at night, on *Finnegans Wake*, she could hear him laughing to himself. A visitor to Joyce, in the late 1930s, Terence White Gervais, asked him if his book was intended as a blending of music and literature. Joyce answered: "No, it's pure music." It is the "Storiella as she is syung" (267.7–8). On being asked if the work contained levels of meaning, Joyce said: "No, no, it's meant to make you laugh." He told his friend Jacques Mercanton: "I am only an Irish clown, a great joker at the universe." To a drinking companion he once corrected the expression *In vino veritas* to *In risu veritas*. Joyce said he wrote the book as he did: "To keep the critics busy for three hundred years."[4] To the Danish writer Tom Kristensen, Joyce said: "Now they're bombing Spain. Isn't it better to make a great joke instead, as I have done?"[5]

Finnegans Wake is a joke based on a joke. The Irish ballad of Tim Finnegan is a joke made by Finnegan at his own wake, when accidentally doused with whiskey, the water of life, he says: "do ye think I'm dead?"[6] In the *Wake* we find: "Mark Time's Finist Joke" (455.29); time's final (Finist) joke is death. There is: "What boyazhness! Sole shadow shows. Tis jest jibberweek's joke" (565.13–14)—fear of the shadow of death (*bojazn*, Russian "fear"). Also, "Jests, jokes, jigs and jorums for the Wake lent from the properties of the late cemented Mr. T. M. Finnegan" (221.26–27).

"Joke" derives from Latin *jocus* ("jest, joke, game") and is akin to Old Saxon and Old High German *gehan* ("to say, to speak"); it is related to Middle Welsh *leith* ("language"). These meanings go back to Sanskrit

---

2. Joyce, *Selected Letters*, 316.
3. Aristotle, *Parts of Animals*, in *Complete Works* 673a.
4. For Joyce's comments in this paragraph, see Ellmann, *Joyce*, 703.
5. Ibid., 693.
6. Ibid., 544n.

The Metaphysics of *Finnegans Wake*

yācati ("he implores"), which has the sense of speaking. To joke is to speak; when he made a joke, he spoke. The words in the *Wake* impose meanings on each other; no word is intended to have a literal meaning. No word can stand alone; in the beginning is the word and in the end is the word. The famous sentence beginning the *Wake* is the completion of the sentence that is broken off on its last page. Instead of squaring the circle, Joyce has circled the square. In an Easter postcard he wrote to Harriet Shaw Weaver in 1927, when he was in the early stages of conceiving the book, Joyce said: "I am making an engine with only one wheel. No spokes of course. The wheel is a perfect square."[7]

The music of *Finnegans Wake* is in the pun. There are four kinds of puns in this music. Many of Joyce's puns are just puns, because to pun is fun: "lovesoftfun at Finnegans Wake" (607.16) and "Fin for fun!" (297.4). Joyce is often just "Fuddling fun for Fullacan's sake" (531.26). The *Wake* is "a grand funferall" (13.15). There are wordplays on how things are said: "This is a Prooshious gunn" (8.10–11); "How bootifull and how truetowife of her" (11.29).

A second kind of pun or wordplay is Joyce's use of an English word to play on a word in another language. The *Wake* is overrun with "lashons of languages" (29.32) (Hebrew *lašon*: "tongue, speech"), lashings. It is possible to identify sixty-two languages and dialects involved in these wordplays.[8]

A third kind of pun is on the names and personalities of historical figures. Among philosophical figures, Anaxagoras becomes "Inexagoras" (155.32), Aristotle becomes "Harrystotalies" (110.17), Machiavelli becomes "Macchevuole" (89.6) (a play on the Italian *ma che vuole*: what do you expect! But also perhaps on "maccheroni").[9] Among literary figures, Dante, Goethe, and Shakespeare become "Daunty, Gouty and Shopkeeper" (539.6). Among figures in political history, Napoleon becomes "Lipoleumhat" (8.16) and "Mr 'Bonaparte Nolan' under the natecup" (334.9–10) wearing his famous bicorne cap. The British statesman W. E. Gladstone becomes "Mr 'Gladstone Browne' in the toll hut" (334.6–7) (he is also the source of the Gladstone bag). There is Charles Stewart Parnell, who led the Irish Nationalist party in the British Parliament, whose shade haunts the *Wake*, beginning from the play on his name on its first page: "oldparr" (3.17). A

---

7. Joyce, *Selected Letters*, 321.
8. McHugh, *Annotations to Finnegans Wake*, xiv–xv.
9. Verene, *Joyce and the Philosophers*, chap. 2.

census of the figures whose names and personalities are played on, in the *Wake*, runs to more than three hundred pages.[10]

The fourth kind of pun is more limited, and concerns wordplays on the idea of the work itself, the prime example of which is its title: "Finnegan" is *fin* (French: "end"), *fine* (Italian: "end") again. The English word "again" has the sense not only of "repetition" but of "back" or "return" and of "opposite," "against." There is no apostrophe because it is a tale of all "Finnegans." The doubling of the "n" reminds us of the multiple sense of "Timm Finn again's" (93.35); "Finnegan, erse solid man, that the humptyhillhead of himself" (3.19–20).

In *Ulysses* Stephen says: "History is a nightmare from which I am trying to awake."[11] In *Finnegans Wake*, "the lingerous longerous book of the dark" (251.24), we enter the nightmare and find that our response can be that the nightmare is just a "nightmaze" (411.8), that is, a great joke. We can make sense of history only as a kind of non-sense, that is, a kind of sense that cannot be reduced to a knowledge of the causes of what is in the maze. The maze is a coincidence of opposites, not a series of causes.

The time we are in, in the world of the dark, is not teleological; it is circular, so that our way in is also our way out, as Joyce says of the Museyroom: "Mind your hats goan in!" (8.9). "Mind your boots goan out" (10.22–23). One thing coincides with another; everything doubles-up like the double meaning of a pun. We are always in Dublin, and we should not "Shun the Punman!" (93.13) if we wish to find our way in this "book of Doublends Jined" (20.15–16). As the French critic Louis Gillet wrote: "Of course, it is no longer a question of Time and Space in this indivisible duration where the absolute reigns. These two comrades, who did their cooking for so long on the scrap-iron stove of Kantian categories, find their pot knocked over by a kick from James Joyce. Their soup is spilled out—chronology disappears and all the centuries are contemporary."[12]

What happens in the *Wake*, as in the world, has happened before and will happen again: "The seim anew" (215.23). All is connected to all in a "chaosmos" (118.21). Joyce's method of composition mirrors this chaosmos. As he told Jacques Mercanton: "Chance furnishes me what I need. I am like a man who stumbles along; my foot strikes something, I bend over,

---

10. Glasheen, *Third Census of Finnegans Wake*, 1–314.
11. Joyce, *Ulysses*, 28.
12. Gillet, *Claybook*, 66.

The Metaphysics of *Finnegans Wake*

and it is exactly what I want."[13] Without a sense of irony, without being schooled in the joke, we may give up exploring the *Wake*, and conclude that it is "usylessly unreadable" (179.26–27). But if we understand the ironic sense of things and have learned, to some extent, not to take ourselves seriously, we can willingly enter the "dreamoneire" (280.1) of Joyce's "édition de ténèbres" (179.27), and read on.

When we read on we pass to the other side of ourselves and come close to the time of origin, in which all is possible. No Virgil or Beatrice awaits to be our guide. We must summon up all the languages we know and all the learning we have. To take us through the text, a "loot of learning" (108.7) is required, and we wonder: "Are we speachin d'anglas landage or are you sprakin sea Djoytsch?" (485.12–13). At the least it is best if we know the major languages Joyce knew in addition to English—Italian, French, German, and Latin. We need not know all the languages that appear in the *Wake*. Joyce said to Mercanton: "Isn't it arbitrary of me to make use, as I do, of forty tongues I don't know in order to express the dream state?"[14] Joyce's answer was, it is arbitrary, but necessary.

We need to know not only the languages but also the books at the *Wake*, out of which it arises and through which it carries its meanings.[15] The whole Western and Asian canons are here. All the great works are awakened in the *Wake*. Little or nothing seems forgotten. They all become vehicles of Joyce's great book, and we see each differently through Joyce's "earsighted view" (143.9–10).

But if we do not know languages and do not read the canon there is no place for us at the *Wake*. We wander in like an uninvited guest to an event we do not understand. No one tells us we have to leave, but we likely will not stay long. Besides languages and the great books, the *Wake* presupposes its readers have what at one time would have been a grammar-school education in English—a good vocabulary, including phonetic ability, knowledge of grammar and punctuation, and the ability to spell. Without a grasp of how things should be said or written, Joyce's wordplays have no effect.

If we know something of Dublin and of Irish history, it is likely all to the good, because Joyce carried Dublin and Ireland in his mind and his psyche at all times. But when Heinrich Straumann, Professor of English Literature at the University of Zurich, asked Joyce if a knowledge of Dublin

---

13. Mercanton, "The Hours of James Joyce," 213.
14. Ibid.
15. Atherton, *Books at the Wake*.

would be useful to read *Finnegans Wake*, Joyce replied: "One should not pay any particular attention to the allusions to place-names, historical events, literary happenings and personalities, but let the literary phenomenon affect one as such."[16] It is no doubt good advice. When listening to music, one should listen. Joyce has given us a work that should be read aloud and that is "Acomedy of letters!" (425.24). Taking the book in hand, we can say to ourselves: "Now, to be on anew and basking again in the panorama of all flores of speech" (143.3–4). We can, with a light heart, follow all the courses and recourses until we come to "A way a lone a last a loved a long the" (628.15–16.)

Aquinas. . . Bruno. Vico. . Joyce

Having set *Finnegans Wake* before us, face-to-face, how might we apply philosophy to it? What might be found in Joyce's great text such that we might have a philosophical understanding *of* it as a work of literature? Professor Straumann said, of his meeting with Joyce, which occurred not long before Joyce died, that he had "an expression of friendly irony," and led their conversation "with a certain light objectivity, as one who has a perfectly well defined attitude towards most things but who is quite ready to revise his thinking with regard to their relationship to each other; almost more like a philosopher than an artist."[17] We may take the approach of philosophy *of* literature, attempting to bring forth, from the *Wake*, its philosophical significance.

Three philosophers are principally to be associated with *Finnegans Wake*. They were born within a few miles of each other, in different centuries. Thomas Aquinas (1224–1274) was born in Roccasecca, near Naples. He studied liberal arts at the University of Naples and, having spent a good portion of his professional life at the University of Paris, returned to Naples at the end of his life, to teach at the University and to preach a series of notable sermons. Giordano Bruno (1584–1600) was born in Nola, some twenty miles east of Naples. He called himself "The Nolan." After spending much of his controversial career in northern Europe and England, he returned to Italy, where he was arrested in Venice and imprisoned by the Inquisition. He was burned at the stake for heresy, in the Campo dei Fiori, in Rome.

16. Straumann, "Last Meeting with Joyce," 114.
17. Ibid.

The Metaphysics of *Finnegans Wake*

Giambattista Vico (1668–1744) was born in the center of Naples. Unlike Aquinas and Bruno he never left Naples, except to serve an early position as tutor to the children of the Rocca family, at Vatolla, in the Cilento, south of Naples. He was Professor of Latin Eloquence at the University of Naples from age thirty-one to age seventy-three. A Venetian edition of his major work, *La Scienza nuova*, was blocked by the Holy Office, but when it was published in Naples no charges were ever brought against him. His contemporary, Pietro Giannone, because of the critical views expressed in his work on the history of Naples, was forced into exile.

In the title of this section I have put Aquinas in the place occupied by Dante in the title of Samuel Beckett's famous essay.[18] The *Divine Comedy* might be seen as the literary alternative to reading the metaphysics and moral philosophy of Thomas Aquinas. Beckett's placement of Dante reminds us that as *Ulysses* has a basis in Homer's poem, so *Finnegans Wake* has a basis in Dante's poem. Dante is the "Tuscan Homer," as Vico called him.[19] Vico's *Scienza nuova* is the specific philosophical work on which *Finnegans Wake* is based, but Aquinas is always there, with Dante, in Joyce's conception of it.

William York Tindall, in his guide to the *Wake*, rightly observes that "Joyce devoted the *Wake* to *quidditas* or Thomistic whatness—the whatness of mankind."[20] The central character of Joyce's work, H. C. Earwicker, is everyman, a "general omnibus character" (444.2). He is, furthermore, "some imparticular who will somewherise for the whole" (602.7). He is "An imposing everybody he always indeed looked, constantly the same as and equal to himself and magnificently well worthy of any and all such universalization" (32.19–21). H.C.E. is everybody and somebody. In philosophical terms, the problem Joyce is posing in the character of H.C.E. is that of "quiddity." It is a problem Joyce takes over from his study of Aquinas.

Joyce regarded Aquinas as the greatest philosopher. To one of the students he tutored in English, in Trieste, during the period when he was completing *A Portrait*, he said he read Aquinas in Latin—a page a day. He told another that he regarded Aquinas as greater than Kant, Schopenhauer, or Nietzsche, and that the reasoning of Aquinas was "like a sharp sword."[21]

---

18. Beckett, "Dante... Bruno. Vico.. Joyce." For a discussion of this essay, see Verene, *Joyce and the Philosophers*, chap. 1.

19. Vico, *New Science*, par. 786.

20. Tindall, *Reader's Guide to Finnegans Wake*, 14.

21. Ellmann, *Joyce*, 342.

The Philosophy of Literature

Just before he left Dublin in 1904, the year he began work on *A Portrait*, Joyce saw himself as "steeled in the school of old Aquinas."[22] In *Stephen Hero*, in the discussion of aesthetics in chapter 19, is the line: "Aquinas is certainly on the side of the capable artist."[23] In *A Portrait*, Stephen presents his theory of the necessary phases of artistic apprehension by paraphrasing the famous definition of beauty from the *Summa Theologica*: "Aquinas says: *ad pulcritudinem tria requiruntur, integritas, consonantia, claritas*. I translate it so: *Three things are needed for beauty, wholeness, harmony and radiance*."[24]

Having elaborated the meanings of each of these features of the aesthetically perceived object, Stephen concludes: "You see that it is that thing which it is and no other thing. The radiance of which he speaks is the scholastic *quidditas*, the *whatness* of a thing. This supreme quality is felt by the artist when the esthetic image is first conceived in his imagination."[25] The perceiver of the artwork comes to its *quidditas* last. The maker of the artwork apprehends its *quidditas* as the moment of its inspiration.

Stephen then claims that art necessarily divides itself according to these three forms of apprehension. He says: "These forms are: the lyrical form, the form wherein the artist presents his image in immediate relation to himself; the epical form, the form wherein he presents his image in mediate relation to himself and to others; the dramatic form, the form wherein he presents his image in immediate relation to others."[26] If we apply this prescient remark to Joyce's works, the first or lyrical corresponds to *A Portrait of the Artist as a Young Man*, the second or epical corresponds to *Ulysses*, and the third or dramatic corresponds to *Finnegans Wake*. A great joke is dramatic, as it is something told by the maker of the joke to others, and the joke itself is dramatic in its form—juxtaposing one thing in relation to another to produce a reaction.

To comprehend Joyce's interest in quiddity requires us to have it in mind as a philosophical principle. *Quidditas* is a term introduced in the translations of Aristotle's works into Latin from Arabic, in the twelfth century, corresponding to the Aristotelian expression *to ti ein einai* (*quod quid*

---

22. Joyce, "The Holy Office," in *Critical Writings*, 152.
23. Joyce, *Stephen Hero*, 96.
24. Joyce, *A Portrait*, 229. The passage in *Summa Theologica* is Part I, question 39, article 9.
25. Joyce, *A Portrait*, 231.
26. Ibid., 232.

The Metaphysics of *Finnegans Wake*

erat esse), "the what it is to be," and having the significance of "essence." In his *Commentary on the Metaphysics of Aristotle*, Aquinas says: "that substance itself is said to be a being of itself, because terms which simply signify substance designate what this thing is. But other classes of things are said to be beings, not because they have a quiddity of themselves... but because 'they belong to such a being,' i.e., because they have some connection with substance, which is a being of itself." The being of something is its essence, which is its substance. Whatever may be said to belong to a thing is not its substance. "For they do not signify quiddity, since some of them are clearly qualities of such a being, i.e. of substance, other quantities, other affections, or something of the sort signified by the other genera."[27]

In his *Metaphysics*, as Aquinas notes, Aristotle says: "The term *substance* is used chiefly of four things, if not of more; for the essence (or quiddity) and the universal and the genus seem to be the substance of each thing, and fourthly the subject. Now the subject is that of which the others are predicated, while it itself is not predicated of anything else."[28] That substance is linguistically subject allows for the Aristotelian conception of definition *per genus et differentiam*. The principle of this definition is the elicitation of the objective intension of the thing being defined—the essential property or properties that all members of the extension of a given class actually have in common. For Aristotle's essentialism there can be definitions only of universals. Thus there are no individual essences.

Aquinas writes, in commenting on Aristotle's description of what an essence is: "it must be noted that by the phrase *to be this* or *being this* he understands the essence of a thing; for example, by *to be man* or *being man* he understands what pertains to the essence of man." But if certain distinctive attributes are predicated of a given man they are not part of the man's essence. "Now the whatness of 'being musical,' i.e., the very essence of musical has nothing to do with your whatness. For if one were to ask what you are, one could not answer that you are musical. Hence it follows that being you is not being musical, because those things which pertain to the quiddity of music are extrinsic to your quiddity, although musical may be predicated of you."

The property of "musical" may be highly distinctive of who you are, and you would be a very different human being without your musical nature, but you would remain a human being. "And this is so because 'you are

27. Aquinas, *Commentary*, 2:490.
28. Ibid., 2:495.

not musical essentially," since musical is not predicated of you essentially but accidentally." Your musical nature is something that can be removed or acquired; it is not your substance. "Therefore what you are 'essentially' pertains to your whatness, because it is predicated of you essentially and not accidentally; for example, man, animal, substance, rational, sensible, and other attributes of this kind, all of which belong to your whatness, are predicated of you essentially."[29] These essential properties constitute the objective intension of the definition of you as a human being and are the universals you share with all others in the extension of the class of human beings.

It is here that a problem arises. How does this substance-based metaphysics account for genuine individuality? If one human being is essentially the same as any other, they are identical; their differences are solely accidental. A real difference between individuals requires a difference in form, that is, in being, an ontological difference. If we think of Socrates's arguments for immortality in the *Phaedo*, his claim is not that he will survive death as a universal human soul (*psyche*) but that the soul of Socrates will pass into the other world. We apprehend ourselves as having an essence separate from our bodies, and in this sense we perceive ourselves not simply as varying from other individuals in terms of our accidental circumstances and abilities but, like Socrates, as having an individual psyche that is part of, yet distinct from, the human psyche generally.

The problem that the Aristotelian conception of quiddity poses for individuality led Duns Scotus to formulate the principle of *haecceitas* (haecceity), a term coined from the adjective *haec*, which indicates a particular thing, a "this." "Haecceity" designates individuality determined as an "ultimate reality of being" that is opposite to a common nature (composed of matter and form) as a particular entity, *ad esse hanc rem*. Haecceity is intended to explain the existence of the individual as originating from common nature that is as such universal and indifferent to individuality. Haecceity is intended to refer to what makes something be a reality ultimately different from any other thing.

Haecceity is no more than the acknowledgement as a metaphysical term that there is real individuality. As a principle it does not explain how an individual essence or quiddity is derived from the essence or substance of an *infima species*. When Joyce, in the statement Stephen makes, quoted above, describes *quidditas* as the *whatness* of a thing, he is speaking

29. Ibid., 2:506.

more from the Scotian conception of haecceity than from the Thomistic-Aristotelian conception of quiddity.

But Joyce's association of this principle with the artwork is of fundamental significance because the artwork offers an example of an object that is different from any other object. The artwork seems to be an *infima species* of its own. No two works of art are the same, yet all have the essential properties of *integritas*, *consonantia*, and *claritas*. It is only when we recognize the "radiance" of a given artwork that we grasp it as original. This sense of the work is what the true artist grasps immediately. Anyone who has a real ability to write poetry knows that a poem does not start with an idea. It starts with the appearance out of nowhere of a metaphor that immediately shines forth as a new being, something the ancients recognized as a visit from the Muses—what issues from the treasure house of memory. The poem develops metaphors from the metaphor. The lyric, Joyce says, as was quoted above, is "the form wherein the artist presents his image in immediate relation to himself."

Joyce's sense of quiddity as the heart of the artwork, which he extrapolates from Aquinas, does not leave his imagination. It remains a concern in *Finnegans Wake*. In philosophical terms, the problem he addresses in *Finnegans Wake* is how the main characters that populate it are at once human types and individuals, including himself as he appears as "Shem the Penman" (125.23), along with Vico as "Shaun the Post" (206.11). In *Finnegans Wake* he must "twist the penman's tale posterwise" (483.2–3). Joyce is at a distance in the *Wake*, portraying himself not in the personal terms of autobiography but in the guise of Shem, the forger of puns, to take the reader into his words and his world. The *Wake* itself is a unique object. There has been nothing like it before and there will be nothing to succeed it in future. It is a this.

Opposites and Cycles

Joyce's other two philosophers, Bruno and Vico, also appear in *A Portrait*, although not so prominently as does Aquinas. In one of the journal entries with which the work ends, Stephen records an exchange he had with his teacher Rev. Charles Ghezzi, SJ, concerning Bruno: "He said Bruno was a terrible heretic. I said he was terribly burned. He agreed to this with some sorrow."[30] Joyce may have read very little of Bruno's actual writings. His

---

30. Joyce, *A Portrait*, 271.

knowledge of Bruno has a source in Isabella Frith's *Life of Giordano Bruno the Nolan* (1887), a work from which Joyce paraphrases a line in his article "The Day of the Rabblement" (1901). His opening line is: "No man, said the Nolan, can be a lover of the true or the good unless he abhors the multitude, and the artist, though he may employ the crowd, is very careful to isolate himself."[31]

He also discussed J. Lewis McIntyre's *Giordano Bruno* in a review titled "The Bruno Philosophy" (1903). In it he says Bruno's "life reads like a heroic fable" and he says "a martyr burned at the stake in the Campo dei Fiori—Bruno, through all these modes and accidents (as he would have called them) of being, remains a consistent spiritual unity."[32] It was Bruno himself who impressed Joyce very much, along with Bruno's general principle of the coincidence of opposites. There are also references to the titles of Bruno's major works in *Finnegans Wake*.[33]

Joyce came to know of Vico during his university studies. Constantine Curran, his school friend, reports that one of the assigned readings of Joyce's college course in 1901 was Raffaello Fornaciari's *Disegno storico della letteratura italiana*. Curran says: "The references to Bruno and to Vico, to the intuitional and pantheistic mode of Bruno's thinking; to the indeterminate encyclopedic sweep of mind which makes Vico, as Fornaciari says, an inexhaustible mine for future quarrying, are sufficient to set an intelligience less alert than Joyce's upon inquiry."[34] While living in Trieste, Joyce resided in via Donato Bramante at the Piazza Giambattista Vico, an address he chose deliberately. One of the students to whom he gave English lessons, Paolo Cuzzi, reports that he discovered Joyce had a passionate interest in Vico.[35]

In 1914, the year Joyce completed *A Portrait*, the first volume of the great Laterza edition of Vico's works appeared. In it was Vico's *De antiquissima Italorum sapientia*, the work containing Vico's famous assertion, *verum esse ipsum factum*, "the true is the same as the made." Vico makes the distinction between *scientia*, in which what is true is so because we make it, and *conscientia*, the "witnessing consciousness" that allows us to recognize what is begotten by divine making. Stephen's last words in *A Portrait* are: "I go to encounter for the millionth time the reality of experience and to forge

---

31. Joyce, "Day of the Rabblement," in *Critical Writings*, 69.
32. Joyce, "The Bruno Philosophy," in *Critical Writings*, 133.
33. See Verene, *Joyce and the Philosophers*, chap. 3.
34. Curran, *Joyce Remembered*, 121.
35. Ellmann, *Joyce*, 340.

The Metaphysics of *Finnegans Wake*

in the smithy of my soul the uncreated conscience of my race." Vico's two principles are merged. Then: "Old father, old artificer, stand me now and ever in good stead."[36] The old artificer is Daedalus, but Vico is also the old artificer who makes the science of the human race from its ancient origins which, once witnessed, will stand in good stead those who can make it again. There is no way to know if Joyce has Vico, the old father, in mind, but the *Scienza nuova* does show us how to forge in the smithy of our souls the uncreated conscience of our race.

In a letter of 1925, Joyce commented to Harriet Shaw Weaver that Bruno's "philosophy is a kind of dualism—every power in nature must evoke an opposite in order to realize itself and opposition brings reunion etc etc."[37] Bruno appears with Vico in the first sentence of the *Wake* (3.2). Vico appears in his Latin name "vicus." Bruno appears in a greater disguise, in the word preceding Vico—"commodius vicus." A commode or chamber pot is a "jordan" (Italian: Giordano), Bruno's first name. A jordan is originally a bottle of water brought from the Jordan River by Crusaders or pilgrims, later transferred to mean a pot or vessel used by physicians and alchemists. Two of Bruno's sources are the alchemist Agrippa of Nettesheim and the alchemist and physician Paracelsus. In *Ulysses* there is: "loosing her nightly waters on the jordan."[38] A vico or vicus is not a river but a road, but Vico is connected to the "riverrun" of the Jordan by his given name, Giovanni Battista (John the Baptist), the saint who preached and baptized along the Jordan River. Vico, born on June 23rd, was named and baptized on June 24th, the feast day of St. John the Baptist. Vico and Bruno and their ideas are recirculated throughout the pages of the *Wake*.

In one of Bruno's best known works, *Spaccio de la bestia trionfante* (*The Expulsion of the Triumphant Beast*)—*Trionfante di bestia*! (305.15)—we find a statement of the coincidence of opposites or contraries as a principle of both metaphysics and moral philosophy. In its first dialogue Sophia says: "What I wish to infer from that [the physical, mathematical, and moral oppositions in life] is that the beginning, the middle, and the end, the birth, the growth, and the perfection of all that we see, come from contraries, through contraries, into contraries, to contraries. And where there is contrariety, there is action and reaction, there is motion, there is

36. Joyce, *A Portrait*, 275–76.
37. Joyce, *Letters of James Joyce*, 224–25.
38. Joyce, *Ulysses*, 169.

diversity, there is number, there is order, there are degrees, there is succession, there is vicissitude."[39]

In the fifth dialogue of *On the Infinite Universe and Worlds*, Philotheo concludes: "From this coincidence of contraries we deduce that ultimately it is divinely right to say and to hold that contraries are within contraries, wherefore it is not difficult to compass the knowledge that each thing is within every other."[40] In the third dialogue of *Cause, Principle and Unity*, Teofilo says: "Hence, every potency, every act which, in the principle, is (so to speak) enfolded, united and unique, is unfolded, dispersed and multiplied in other things."[41] Each entity, then, is a constant circle of potency and act in which each act becomes a new potency, making itself into a circle or cycle that passes continually beyond itself, always becoming what it is not.

The coincidence of contraries, understood as a circle of potency and act, connects Bruno's metaphysics of nature with Vico's metaphysics of history. Vico regards his new science above all to be a metaphysics: "This New Science or metaphysic [*Cosi questa Nuova Scienza, o sia la metafisica*], studying the common nature of nations in the light of divine providence, discovers the origins of divine and human things among the gentile nations, and thereby establishes a system of the natural law of the gentes." This *ius gentium naturale* is what Vico terms *la storia ideal eterna* (ideal eternal history), which consists of three ages through which all nations pass in their rise, maturity, and fall. "These are: (1) The age of gods, in which the gentiles believed they lived under divine governments, and everything was commanded them by auspices and oracles, which are the oldest matters in profane history. (2) The age of heroes, in which they reigned everywhere in aristocratic republics, on account of a certain superiority of nature which they held themselves to have over the plebs. (3) The age of men, in which all men recognized themselves as equal in human nature, and therefore there were established first the popular republics and then the monarchies, both of which are forms of human government."[42]

These three ages are a cycle or *corso* at the termination of which the nation undergoes a *ricorso*, a repetition of the same three ages.[43] Each of these two *corsi* begins in what Vico calls a "barbarism of sense" (*barbarie del*

---

39. Bruno, *Triumphant Beast*, 90–91.
40. Bruno, *Infinite Universe*, 369.
41. Bruno, *Cause*, 66.
42. Vico, *New Science*, par. 31.
43. For a full exposition of Vico's philosophy, see Verene, *Vico's New Science*.

The Metaphysics of *Finnegans Wake*

senso) and ends in a "barbarism of reflection" (*barbarie della riflessione*).⁴⁴ A *corso* is a nightmare of history in which "Men first feel necessity, then look for utility, next attend to comfort, still later amuse themselves with pleasure, thence grow dissolute in luxury, and finally go mad and waste their substance [*finalmente impazzano e istrappazzar le sostanze*]."⁴⁵

Vico's view is similar to Rousseau's conclusion to his criticism of luxury in his *First Discourse*: "Finally, they chased the gods out in order to live in the temples themselves."⁴⁶ Vico's metaphysics has at its heart the insight that all in experience has a beginning, middle, and end. This cyclic nature of things is writ large in the life of nations and is their common nature. Their ideal eternal history is a providential order. For Vico providence in history is cyclic. In this view he stands against the eighteenth-century view, as found, for example, in Kant, that conceives the workings of providence in history as a progressing toward an end, such that history moves ideally toward perfection.

Joyce restudied Vico to write *Finnegans Wake*. In March 1925, while suffering with his failing eyesight, he wrote to Weaver: "I should like to hear Vico read to me again in the hope that some day I may be able to write again. I put an advertisement in the Mail for a reader but got not even one reply though I have often seen advertisements from Italians in it."⁴⁷ Joyce reportedly told friends and colleagues who wished to understand what he was writing to read Vico's *Scienza nuova*, and, if they did not read Italian, to read Michelet's French translation.

While on a walk with Padraic Colum, in Paris, Joyce said: "I don't take Vico's speculations literally; I use his cycles as a trellis."⁴⁸ A trellis is a structure of latticework for the support of climbing plants. But it is also possible to speak of "a trellis of interlacing streams." One thinks of the many rivers in the *Wake*. Etymologically, "trellis" is a fabric of coarse weave, and specifically, *trilicius* (Vulgar Latin) is "woven with triple thread." "Trellis" has within it the notion of three (*tres*). To Vico's three ages, Joyce adds a fourth—providence: "thunderburst, ravishment, dissolution and providentiality" (362.30–31). Joyce told Professor Straumann: "If a premise to the

---

44. Vico, *New Science*, par. 1106.
45. Ibid., par. 241.
46. Rousseau, *First Discourse*, 54.
47. Joyce, *Letters of Joyce*, 3:117–18.
48. Colum, *Our Friend James Joyce*, 82.

reading of the work must be sought, then it should be a knowledge of the philosopher Giambattista Vico, to whom he was greatly indebted."[49]

There is no divine order in Joyce's cycle. Providence takes its place in the cycle as the moment of its dissolution. In Joyce's "wholemole millwheeling vicociclometer" (614.27) there is "eggburst, eggblend, eggburial and hatch-as-hatch can" (614.32–33). "Providentiality" is the hatching or eggburst that will generate the next turn of the square wheel. The dream will be redreamed. We will awake (our daily Easter) only to go to sleep again (our entrance into the other side of our existence). The metaphysics of the cycle is ironic, for, like the trope of irony, the meaning of what is said lies in the contrary. When one meaning is united with the other, the irony emerges. Metaphysical speech is ironic speech. With his vicociclometer, Joyce has shown us how it works.

Joyce's Speech Acts

Beckett, in his essay on Joyce, says of Joyce's writing: "Here form *is* content, content *is* form. You complain that this stuff is not written in English. It is not written at all. It is not to be read—or rather it is not only to be read. It is to be looked at and listened to. His writing is not *about* something; *it is that something itself*. . . . When the sense is sleep, the words go to sleep (see the end of 'Anna Livia')."[50] The Anna Livia episode ends: "Dark hawks hear us. Night! Night! My ho head halls. I feel as heavy as yonder stone. Told me of John or Shaun? Who were Shem and Shaun the living sons or daughters of? Night now! Tell me, tell me, tell me, elm! Night night! Telmetale of stem or stone. Beside the rivering waters of, hitherandthithering waters of. Night!" (215.36–216.5). The last pages of Anna Livia Plurabelle are the only ones from *Finnegans Wake* that Joyce read aloud as a recording.

Whoever hears Joyce read these last lines can immediately grasp what Beckett means. The words themselves go to sleep as one follows them into "Night!" In his reflections on the writing of poetry, Borges says, of this last line of Anna Livia: "We feel that the line is an invention, a poem—a very complex web, as Stevenson would have had it. And yet I suspect there was a moment when the word 'night' was quite as impressive, was quite as

---

49. Straumann, "Last Meeting with Joyce," 114.
50. Beckett, "Dante. . . Bruno. Vico. . Joyce," 14.

The Metaphysics of *Finnegans Wake*

strange, was quite as awe-striking as this beautiful winding sentence: 'rivering waters of, hitherandthithering waters of, Night!'"[51]

On the first page of the *Wake* is: "nor avoice from afire bellowsed mishe mishe to tauftauf thuartpeatrick" (3.9-10)—"me me" (Irish *mise*: "me") to *taufen* (German: "baptize"). "Thou art Peter" (Matt 16:18). In these lines of Matthew, Jesus says to Peter that "on this rock I will build my church," making a play on words—Peter and rock in Greek (*Petros* and *petra*), thus "peatrick." In "tauftauf" we hear the movement of the water in baptism, the rite upon which the church depends. Once read with an ear to the language, we are immersed in the thing itself and the moving water will keep going through our mind and enter our memory.

Another passage that illustrates Beckett's point is: "The oldold stoliolum! From quiqui quinet to michemiche chelet and a jambebatiste to a brulobrulo!" (117.10-12). Edgar Quinet and Jules Michelet are the French historians who were influenced by, and promoted, Vico's philosophy of history. Their surnames are doubled, as is "oldold." The doubling gives a sense of old—the old, old story is stolid. Joyce plays on Vico's Christian name by combining two French words: *jambe* ("leg") and *batiste* (a type of smooth, sheer fabric). Perhaps this combination is how "Jean Baptiste" might sound, if slightly mispronounced, in French. In this form he takes Vico back to Bruno. In "brulobrulo" we hear the faggots burning in the *supplizio* of Bruno, in which he was "terribly burned." Once we encounter Bruno as "brulobrulo" we always hear it when we think of Bruno. Vico and Bruno tell the old, old story of humanity, and it is retold by Quinet and Michelet. Being told and retold, it solidifies.

Joyce, in the *Wake*, is now retelling it in a particular way: "It is told in sounds in utter that, in signs so adds to, in universal, in polyglutural, in each auxiliary neutral idiom, sordomutics, florilingua, sheltafocal, flayflutter, a con's cubane, a pro's tutute, strassarab, ereperse and anythongne athall" (117.12-16). It is told in *Wake* in any way it can be told, in any language, in any way words can be pronounced, in flowery expressions and neutral idioms, by deaf mutes and prostitutes, in any tongue, by anyone at all who speaks in the great hall of history. Joyce has found a way to speak that has never been found before.

Beckett characterizes the world of the *Wake* as corresponding to Dante's *Purgatorio*. He says that in this world: "There is an endless verbal germination, maturation, putrefaction, the cyclic dynamism of the

---

51. Borges, *Craft of Verse*, 88-89.

intermediate." The way in which the *Wake* is expressed is cyclic. Words arise, say something, and then double back on themselves. Beckett says: "This reduction of various expressive media to their primitive economic directness, and the fusion of these primal essences into an assimilated medium for the exteriorization of thought, is pure Vico, and Vico applied to the problem of style." The words carry with them their original meanings, such as are explored in the *Cratylus*, Vico's favorite Platonic dialogue. Vico repeatedly establishes his claims by his etymologies.

Beckett continues: "But Vico is reflected more explicitly than by a distillation of disparate poetic ingredients into a synthetical syrup. We notice that there is little or no attempt at subjectivism or abstraction, no attempt at metaphysical generalization. We are presented with a statement of the particular."[52] Joyce's sense of quiddity-haecceity continually directs our attention to the reality of the particular. His language cannot be duplicated, abstracted, or universalized.

Joyce invents language itself, before our eyes and ears. Borges, with *Finnegans Wake* in mind, says: "I have spoken of words standing out at the beginning, when men invented them. I have thought that the word 'thunder' might mean not only the sound but the god."[53] Joyce's famous ten thunder words are expressions of Vichian thunder, in that, in the *New Science*, the thunder that the *giganti* experience for the first time, as the world dries out after the universal flood, is the cause of the first word. Vico says, of the *giganti*, that the appearance of thunder and lightning caused them to raise their eyes to the sky for the first time, and they thought the sky was a great body, "because in that state their nature was that of men all robust bodily strength, who expressed their very violent passions by shouting [*urlando*] and grumbling [*brontolando*], they pictured the sky to themselves as a great animated body, which in that aspect they called Jove, the first god of the so-called greater gentes."[54] Vico uses two special verbs—*urlare* (to howl as an animal and to shout as a human) and *brontolare* (to grumble and to rumble as thunder). The words themselves show the *giganti* to be protohuman. Vico says: "Human words were formed from interjections. . . . In all languages these are monosyllables."[55] Once Jove is named, the *giganti* possess the power of the name, and anything can be named.

52. Beckett, "Dante... Bruno. Vico.. Joyce," 16–17.
53. Borges, *Craft of Verse*, 88.
54. Vico, *New Science*, par. 377.
55. Ibid., par. 448.

The Metaphysics of *Finnegans Wake*

Jove is the central figure of poetic metaphysics that precedes rational metaphysics. Vico says: "So that, as rational metaphysics teaches that man becomes all things by understanding them (*homo intelligendo fit omnia*), this imaginative metaphysics [*metafisica fantasticata*] shows that man becomes all things by *not* understanding them (*homo non intelligendo fit omnia*)."[56] Behind all language there is a common mental dictionary or a common mental language (*dizionario mentale* or *lingua mentale comune*). In it are the origins of "all the diverse articulated languages."[57] In it is the common sense of humanity, of the great city of the human race. This language is wholly mental. It can be expressed only by the various languages. Each is drawn from it as if from the *topoi* of human memory. When we take words back to their original meanings we come close to it. The speech of *Finnegans Wake* is the attempt to bring forth this language of all languages to the extent that we can think it. The *New Science* describes it; *Finnegans Wake* attempts to speak it to the extent that such is possible. In so doing, the words become the things they mean. At least its speech from time to time accomplishes this, and forges for us the conscience of our race. Closer we cannot come.

In Vico's conception of poetic logic is the solution to the metaphysical problem of quiddity—the form of a particular universal, what Vico terms the imaginative universal (*universale fantastico*). It is the product of *fantasia*, not of rational thought. *Fantasia* is the "making imagination." Before human beings can grasp the world as a rationally understood object, they make their world through the power of the image. Vico says a metaphor is a fable in brief, and "These fables are ideal truths suited to the merit of those of whom the vulgar tell them; and such falseness to fact as they contain consists simply in failure to give their subjects their due. So that, if we consider the matter well, poetic truth is metaphysical truth, and physical truth which is not in conformity with it should be considered false."[58] Furthermore, the fables have "univocal, not analogical, meanings for various particulars comprised under their poetic genera."[59]

Thus we can say that Jove is in all things. The gods that are all things are all equally Jove, and Jove is Jove. And we can in like manner say all courageous warriors are each equally Achilles, and in addition Achilles is Achilles

---

56. Ibid., par. 405.
57. Ibid., par. 145.
58. Ibid.. par. 205.
59. Ibid., par. 210.

(as discussed in chapter 1, herein). This manner of concept-formation is open to the imagination but closed to reason. Individuals are individuals and also universals—human types. The parallel in rational thought is that the property of divinity can be univocally, not analogically, predicated of all gods, and the virtue of courage can be univocally predicated of all warriors.

It is in the imagination or *fantasia* that the problem raised by Joyce's sense of quiddity is resolved. Now we can understand how H. C. Earwicker is both himself and the universalization of himself as Here Comes Everybody. In *Finnegans Wake* Joyce intends to write the logic and language of Vico's *universali fantastici*. In the dream our conscience is taken back to the speech of the origin. All we can do is read along, with "two thinks at a time" (583.7), and allow language to be what it means, in the sense that a poem must not mean but be. *Finnegans Wake* shows its "reader" how this claim can be true. And we find that doing so is "lot's of fun."

How language represents the world is an abiding concern of philosophers. Attention to how Joyce uses language is of philosophical importance, in regard to his ability to have the expression itself *be* the thing meant. Philosophers of language have often maintained that the structure of language can represent the nature of reality. In so claiming they have assumed that the purpose of any sentence is to describe or "picture" the actual state of things. J. L. Austin challenged the view that indicative sentences are simply devices for making statements.[60] The contribution to speech act theory, for which Austin is most known, is the conception of "explicit performative utterances." These sentences, unlike sentences that assert a given state of affairs or describe some fact, are neither true nor false, as are "constatives."

Performatives take the form of assertions, such as "I promise," "apologize," or "request." Any sentence that is followed by an illocutionary verb can be regarded as a performative. In promising, for example, one is making a promise, not stating that one is making it. One is making explicit what one is doing, and this is different from describing what is being done or claiming that one is doing it. We might hold that what such performatives mean is dependent upon conventional understandings of them in a given community. What they mean is what, in such a community, they are taken to mean. Peformatives, then, are a certain kind of conventional speech act. Although convention is relevant to the success of performative statements, more fundamental to them is not their meaning within a given community but recognition of the intention implicit in the performative.

---

60. Austin, *How to Do Things with Words*.

The Metaphysics of *Finnegans Wake*

Beckett's claim that Joyce's writing "is not *about* something; *it is that something itself*" is close to Austin's general conception of a performative. To promise is a self-contained speech act. What it says is also what it does. Its form is its content. Whether the person follows through on the promise, or whether what is promised is relevant, or even makes sense, is not part of the performative. But Joyce's "performatives" are well beyond Austin's examples. By taking words back to their origin, where the words are what the things themselves are, Joyce, following Vico and expanding on Vico's procedure, makes all language performative before it becomes constative. When we hear the "hitherandthithering waters of. Night!" we are in the Night. Night is; it is neither true nor false. It is not a statement of fact; it is the fact. When Vico gives us the word "Jove," made out of thunder and the onomatopoia of its sound, we are at the being of the first word. The first page of the *Wake* is full of father-words. When we hear the water sounds of "tauftauf" or the fire sounds of "brulobrulo" we are hearing the phenomena that is indistinguishable from the word as first formed.

I do not mean that every word and every phrase or expression in the *Wake* holds this bond between form and content and origin, but Joyce's ability to do these things with words is what gives *Finnegans Wake* its language, and it is what makes it unreadable. For to be readable, the words of the *Wake* would need to have meanings that were already finished and understood. Instead we encounter words that are making their own meanings and their own truth, and there is nothing we can do about it. The more we interpret the *Wake*—attempt to work out its narrative, to articulate the hidden meanings of its words, unpack its characters, formulate its intentions—the further we get from entering into this new form of literature, formed from litter and letter, that has no beginning, middle, or end.

We should accept the judgment of Danis Rose and John O'Hanlon, the editors of the corrected edition of *Finnegans Wake*, that "James Joyce's *Finnegans Wake* represents the summit of twentieth-century literary production in the English language." And we should follow their kind advice: "Gentle reader, were you to ask *How should I read this book*? We would answer: passively, like any good book, neither too fast nor too slow. Do not pause because you cannot understand a word or words: you are not expected to understand it all. Imagine yourself a child, leaning over the banisters, listening to the grown-up banter going on below. You are learning a language: a night language. Morning will come and the clouds of unknowing will begin to dissipate."[61] Indeed, we will then go "past Morningtop's necessity and Harington's invention, to the clarience of the childlight in the studiorium upsturts" (266.11–13), only to think again how we might enter the *Wake*'s world, a world in which the words are the things they mean.

---

61. Rose and O'Hanlon, "Preface," *Finnegans Wake*, 7–8.

3

The Politics of *The People, Yes*

The Idea of Yes

When America was becoming America, two poets caught its voice: Walt Whitman, *Leaves of Grass* (1855) and Carl Sandburg, *Smoke and Steel* (1920). We may add to these the New England voice of Robert Frost and, today, the Nebraska voice of Ted Kooser, thirteenth Poet Laureate of the United States. Carl Sandburg was born and raised in Galesburg, Illinois, 150 miles southwest of Chicago, the "Hog Butcher for the World," and "City of Big Shoulders." He spent the last part of his career at Flat Rock, North Carolina, in a former plantation house and farm called Connemara, where his wife Paula bred champion goats, a herd of nearly 100—now a national historic site.[1] His birthplace in Galesburg is an Illinois State historic site. The middle Midwest and the middle South form a continuum. They both have their own way of speaking and share some phrases; they eat the same food, they practice their own sense of humor, and they have a deep awareness of the civic.

Sandburg wrote an autobiographical novel about Galesburg, *Always the Young Strangers*, capturing the uniqueness of the place of his youth and the world of his parents, both Swedish immigrants. His father worked all his life as a laborer in the yards of the Chicago, Burlington, and Quincy Railroad, the headquarters of which was in Galesburg. In 1957, when asked

---

1. Niven, *Sandburg*, pt. 4.

The Philosophy of Literature

by reporters what he wanted out of life, Sandburg said: "All my life, I've been thinking what I want out of life."[2] He told Edward R. Murrow: "What I need mainly is three things in life, possibly four: To be out of jail, to eat regular, to get what I write printed, and then a little love at home and a little outside."[3] His physician and old friend, having given him a physical examination when he was 79, noted that Sandburg's health "was all to the good." It was his reply to Sandburg, who had pounded on his stomach and said, "How's that, doc?"[4] When he died, ten years later, Sandburg's ashes were brought back to his Galesburg birthplace.

Sandburg took up the credo in Whitman's "Starting from Paumanok": "I am the credulous man of qualities, ages, races. I advance from the people in their own spirit." In *The People, Yes*, Sandburg said: "I am credulous about the destiny of man and I believe more than I can ever prove of the future of the human race."[5] Sandburg believed in democracy and the American Dream.

Sandburg was a poet's poet. There was a time when nearly every schoolchild in America had read his six-line haiku-like poem "Fog," and could quite likely recite its first two lines regarding the fog and little cat feet.[6] Unlike Joyce, Sandburg did not write in relation to the work of any particular philosophers. As much as Joyce was an Irish-European, Sandburg was a Swedish heritage-American. Sandburg was also a historian. He was awarded the Pulitzer Prize for his biography of Lincoln. He was later awarded the Pulitzer Prize for his *Complete Poems*. Sandburg was expected by many to one day receive the Nobel Prize, but he never did. He thought his language likely was "too Americanese" for the Nobel Committee. He told his publisher, Harcourt, that "too much of my language . . . might seem almost nationalistic in its flaunting of the North American airs and syllables."[7]

Both John Steinbeck and Ernest Hemingway, on receiving the Nobel Prize, were quoted as saying it should have gone to Sandburg. When Hemingway won the Nobel Prize for literature in 1954, he said: "I would have been most happy to know that the prize had been awarded to Carl

---

2. Ibid., 656.
3. Ibid., 632.
4. Ibid., 655.
5. Ibid., 704. Quoted by Niven.
6. Sandburg, *Complete Poems*, 33.
7. Niven, *Sandburg*, 489.

The Politics of *The People, Yes*

Sandburg." Sandburg telegraphed him: "Your unprecedented comment on the award deeply appreciated and understood if only as fellowship between two Illinois boys."[8] Hemingway was born in the Chicago suburb of Oak Park.

Although Sandburg is not a "philosophical" poet in any obvious sense, within his poetry are ideas and insights of great value to philosophy. Philosophy is *in* his poetry. George Santayana says: "The vision of philosophy is sublime. The order it reveals in the world is something beautiful, tragic, sympathetic to the mind, and just what every poet, on a small or large scale, is always trying to catch."[9] These things are just what Sandburg is trying to catch in the American spirit, in the American sense of the people as the heart of politics—the people, coming from Latin *populus*, connected to Greek *plethos*: "throng," "a multitude." The people can be the plebs, the *hoi polloi*, the many. They are the basis of politics; without the people there is no politics. There is no *polis* from which to have politics.

"Yes" is a word held in common by Joyce and Sandburg. It is the word that runs through Molly Bloom's soliloquy and the last word of *Ulysses*. It is the last word of Sandburg's title *The People, Yes* that is repeated at various points in the work and that gains our attention when we come to it. "Yes" is a completely English word, from Middle English and Old English. "Yes" is affirmation, agreement, in ordinary speech. As the last word of *Ulysses* it stands alone, capitalized. As the key word of the title of Sandburg's work it tells us the status of the people. In both instances, "Yes" stands alone; there is no way to encompass it. It is out of time and out of space. It is absolute and reassuring. There is no way to qualify it. If it is an answer, we do not know quite what the question is. Once "Yes" is said, all remains thus and so.

Who were the people who made up the "Yes"? They were always the young strangers, who followed the railroad to Illinois and on West, pursuing opportunity, as America realized itself. Sandburg's art was to listen to their language. As he says in his autobiographical novel: "This small town of Galesburg, as I look back on it, was a piece of the American Republic. Breeds and blood stains that figure in history were there for me, as a boy, to see and hear in their faces and their ways of talking and activity."[10] Sandburg asked himself: "What is this America I am a part of, where I will soon be a full citizen and a voter? All of us are living under the American flag, the

---

8. Ibid., 635.
9. Santayana, *Three Philosophical Poets*, 10.
10. Sandburg, *Young Strangers*, 280.

Stars and Stripes—what does it mean? Men have died for it—why? When they say it is a free country, they mean free for what and free for whom, and what is freedom?" He says: "Those questions in those words may not have run through my mind yet they ran in my blood. Dark and tangled they were to run in my blood for many years. To some of the questions I would across the years get only half-answers, mystery answers."[11]

The American Dream is the other side of Joyce's dream of the *Wake*. Both dreams are real: two halves of human existence. In *Remembrance Rock*, his more than one-thousand-page novel about the development of the American Dream, Sandburg begins with: "Time eats all things. The brown gold of autumn says so. The falling leaves in the last rainwind before the first spit of snow—they have their way of saying, Listen, be quiet, winter comes: Time eats all things."[12] Joyce's time and Sandburg's time are of a piece. Time comes back on itself in our "nightmaze" and in the "nightmaze" of history as we find ourselves in it.

In the second of his thirty-eight definitions of poetry that preface his poems in *Good Morning, America*, Sandburg says: "Poetry is an art practiced with the terribly plastic material of language."[13] Joyce listens to many languages, and we listen with him in his "dreamoneire." Sandburg listened to the American language until it became his poetry, and, like Joyce, he had a sense of humor that appears in every corner of his words. Sandburg says: "This face you got, this here phizzog you carry around." He says: "Somebody slipped it to you and it was like a package marked: 'No goods exchanged after being taken away.'"[14]

For Joyce and Sandburg, we find ourselves here in the world and in language. What can we do but make the best of it? For that we need a sense of humor. And we need a way to see ourselves. That is our freedom. Sandburg's first definition of poetry is: "Poetry is a projection across silence of cadences arranged to break that silence with definite intentions of echoes, syllables, wave lengths."[15] Joyce's unique poetry of *Finnegans Wake* records the words of many dialects, and spells words and phrases the way they are said. We recognize them from having heard them.

---

11. Ibid., 287.
12. Sandburg, *Remembrance Rock*, 33.
13. Sandburg, *Complete Poems*, 317.
14. Ibid., 396.
15. Ibid., 317.

The Politics of *The People, Yes*

Sandburg's epic, free-verse poem of *The People, Yes* takes no liberties in its incorporations of peoples' speech. For the reader who has listened to the speech of Middle America, what is on the page rings true with startling exactness. It is a language of expressions that are rapidly disappearing, with the onset of the media-speech of newscasts, talk shows, and sitcoms, as well as the fractured words of electronic exchanges between individuals. As mentioned earlier, Joyce's text becomes unfathomable with the abridgement of literary knowledge and the disappearance of grammar-school education, replaced by the "sordomutics" of the modern classroom, with its instruction not done in "anythongue athall," students dutifully seated at computers, heads bowed as if in one of the "*Blogia*"s of Dante's *Inferno*.

Sandburg's epic is divided into 107 sections, with a prefatory comment on its content, indicating that it is composed of stories, psalms, memoranda, sayings, yarns, "broken by plain and irregular sounds and echoes from the roar and whirl of street crowds, work gangs, sidewalk clamor." He also says it has interludes of the peaceful blue of the sky and stars, but adds that these sights pass "over the phantom frames of skyscrapers."[16] Sandburg is not a rural poet or a city poet. To a great extent he is between them, as a small-town poet. He sees what the farmer sees and he sees what the city worker sees. Ever-present is not only his sense of the joke but also his sense of what is uneven and unfair in social order—his sense of human justice.

Offsetting his sense of the uniqueness of the individual is his concept of the "family of man," which became the title of the book of photographs of the human condition taken by his brother-in-law and close friend Edward Steichen. Steichen's pictorial images were as widespread as Sandburg's poetic images. Joyce's "essay on man" that is *Finnegans Wake* is also a version of the family of man, done in European terms. In their different ways, Joyce and Sandburg take humanity as their subject matter.

At Sandburg's memorial service in September, 1967, organized by Chief Justice Earl Warren, at the Lincoln Memorial in Washington, nearly six thousand people gathered to hear poets Mark Van Doren and Archibald MacLeish, among others. Unannounced, President Lyndon Johnson appeared, to express his praise for "this vital, exuberant, wise and gentle man."[17] In his poem "Prairie" Sandburg wrote: "I was born on the prairie and the milk of its wheat, the red of its clover, the eyes of its women, gave

---

16. Ibid., 437.
17. Niven, *Sandburg*, 704.

The Philosophy of Literature

me a song and a slogan."[18] Sandburg said the prairie town of Galesburg burned in his memory. He was, as his book for young readers is titled, a *Prairie-Town Boy*.[19] The prairie can be an Elysian field like the word from which it comes, *pratum*, "meadow," a happy place to dwell.

Padraic Colum, the Irish poet and playwright, the friend of Joyce to whom he made the comment that he used Vico's cycles as a trellis, wrote a statement on the essence of *The People, Yes* that was included on its cover by the publisher in its 1964 reprinting. "The fine thing about *The People, Yes* is that it is indubitable speech. Here is a man speaking, a man who knows all sorts and conditions of men, who can be nice and witty, stirring and nonsensical with them all." The speech Sandburg captures is, without question, accurate, never invented or forced. He and Joyce have different ears, but the same ear.

Colum says further: "If America has a folksinger today he is Carl Sandburg, a singer who comes out of the prairie soil, who has the prairie inheritance, who can hand back to the people a creation that has scraps of their own insight, humor, and imagination." Sandburg is what the Illinois prairie is. His words issue from the heartland of America and the American Dream of the civic of self-determination, of hard work that yields liberty and individuality. Colum concludes: "He has a passion that gives dignity to all he says. It is a passion for humanity, not merely for the man with depths of personality in him, but for the ordinary man and woman."[20] Greatness is apparent in the exceptional, but the dignity and the greatness in the ordinary is what we may learn from the songs and poems of Sandburg. If we can follow his sense of things we can find ourselves and everything around us there, before us, in words.

Sandburg's intention in *The People, Yes* was not to set out a political or economic theory in poetic form.[21] He intended it to be a statement simply of democracy, to show the people to themselves and to show the common dignity of its citizenship, to give their own words back to the people. He held that the most detestable word in the English language is "Exclusive."[22] All that is human is acceptable and is to be accepted. In one of his late poems, his subject is "The Abracadabra Boys"—"their fun is being what

18. Sandburg, *Complete Poems*, 79.
19. Niven, *Sandburg*, 706.
20. Sandburg, *The People, Yes*. See back cover.
21. Niven, *Sandburg*, 504.
22. Ibid., 505.

The Politics of *The People, Yes*

they are, like our fun is being what we are—only they are more sorry for us being what we are than we are for them being what they are."[23] Sandburg says the abracadabra boys point at you, at us, as the rabble, because we "lack jargons." Our language is not their language. Their language is more exclusive. We will say anything and listen to anything that is human.

The People, Yes is Sandburg's address to the American people, showing us, his readers, how to be the people we are. "The people move in a fine thin smoke, the people, yes" (22).[24] Sandburg's epic is an instruction in the pursuit of self-knowledge. If we do not in some way see ourselves in these lines we can realize little or nothing from them. Poetry is a mirror we can hold up to ourselves and, in its images, see our image. Sandburg is an "Imagist" poet. When we begin to see ourselves as human, as part of the people who are us, we can begin to place ourselves as individual versions of humanity in the world. It is a task we cannot put off. As Sandburg reminds us: "Time eats all things." Time is not memory; time is forgetting. Poetry acts against time. It lets us know that we are and what we are. Sandburg says, in his last definition of poetry in his preface to *Good Morning, America*: "Poetry is the capture of a picture, a song, or a flair, in a deliberate prism of words."[25] It is Sandburg's gloss on Horace's famous definition, *Ut pictura poesis*.[26]

Sandburg gives us a picture of what we are when we place ourselves "in a deliberate prism of words." He gives us a self-portrait in his description of a hobo looking for a home, in *The People, Yes* (88). In his younger days, crisscrossing America, he called himself "a migrant roadster." Joyce is the perennial expatriate. Sandburg is the patriot seeking the ground of his patriotism and his place in humanity: "The people is Everyman, everybody. Everybody is you and me and all others" (14). Everybody is also H.C.E., "Here Comes Everybody." We meet everybody in two ways that encompass every way, by passing between *Finnegans Wake* and *The People, Yes*. As *Finnegans Wake* is the culmination of Joyce's career, *The People, Yes* is the culmination of Sandburg's. The poems that come before it build up to it and in some degree are incorporated in it. Those poems that come after its appearance, in 1936, do not move to a new level or style and in many ways

---

23. Sandburg, *Complete Poems*, 643.

24. Sandburg, *The People, Yes*. Here and hereinafter, quotations from this work are cited in the text by the section number.

25. Sandburg, *Complete Poems*, 319.

26. Horace, *Ars poetica*, 361.

continue to echo its themes. For the persistent reader of Sandburg's poetry, *The People, Yes* is everything Sandburg's poetry is.

Human Nature and Human Language

The essence of the human being is rationality. It defines the human being as different from the other animals. In what aspect of the human does this rationality appear? We may say, with Cassirer, in *An Essay on Man*: "instead of defining man as an *animal rationale*, we should define him as an *animal symbolicum*."[27] Human beings are the animals who can use words to create culture, to use words not only to designate things but to use words to define other words and further to use words in "the tracing of the trajectories of a finite sound to the infinite points of its echoes"—as Sandburg says in his fourth definition of poetry in *Good Morning, America*.[28]

Sandburg begins *The People, Yes* with a myth—the myth of the origin of the People and of what is distinctive to the human being—language. He retells the biblical story of the Tower of Babel of Genesis 11: "Now the whole earth had one language and the same words." The families of Noah's sons, Ham, Japheth, and Shem, as they migrated eastward, said to one another: "Come, let us build ourselves a city, and a tower with its top in the heavens, and let us make a name for ourselves; otherwise we shall be scattered abroad upon the face of the whole earth." Sandburg says the people came "From the four corners of the earth." They were "the family of man." They asked: "Where to now? what next?" (1). Thus in the beginning the people asked the question with which Sandburg's poem ends: "Where to? what next?" (102). Sandburg's people, having come together, "wanted to put up something proud to look at." So they began to build a tower "into the top of the sky" (1).

In the Genesis story, the Lord came from the heavens to see the city and the tower that the mortals had built. "And the Lord said, 'Look, they are one people, and they have all one language; and this is only the beginning of what they will do; nothing that they propose to do will now be impossible for them.'" Sandburg says, in the first section of his poem: "the big job got going." Everyone was working together. He says: "God Almighty could have struck them dead or smitten them deaf and dumb." But, he says, "God was a whimsical fixer. God was an understanding Boss" (1). In the Genesis

---

27. Cassirer, *Essay on Man*, 26.
28. Sandburg, *Complete Poems*, 317.

The Politics of *The People, Yes*

story, the Lord says: "'Come, let us go down, and confuse their language there, so that they will not understand one another's speech.' So the Lord scattered them abroad from there over the face of all the earth, and they left off building the city" (11:8).

Sandburg says that God "suddenly shuffled all the languages, changed the tongues of men so they all talked different." The workmen, he says, could not tell each other what tools to use. The masons could not understand what the hod carriers said. The carpenters could not communicate with the helpers. All the different workers and bosses could not communicate "and the job was wrecked." The job could not be finished, thus: "The wreck of it stood as a skull and a ghost." Sandburg says: "Some called it the Tower of Babel job" (1). In the biblical account the people spoke one language and because this ability made them possess a power nearly divine, the Lord realized that to dissolve language into languages would insure that they remained mortal, without the power to connect earth and sky, to merge human and divine. By altering language the Lord altered human nature.

Sandburg's Babel-story points to the fact that in this case the Lord's action was not wrathful but whimsical. In Sandburg's version, the people of the earth, when they assembled, already spoke various languages but they could communicate. But God Almighty simply shuffled the languages. Nothing can be accomplished without the people being able to communicate. Language and work are the two things deeply connected to human nature, and one requires the other. Language is not private, and work is social. The Tower of Babel job could not be completed. The story of the people, of humanity, is the story of its attempt to recover from this dissipation of the origin. Sandburg's story begins, not with the creation of the world but with the creation of the people. In the beginning of the world was the word of God and in the beginning of the people was the word of man.

In the second section of his poem, Sandburg tells another story of the beginning of the people. He proceeds to chronicle the shapes of the people and the individual forms their human nature takes, and these forms are found in their language, the way they speak. In this account all the people in the world assemble on the Midwestern prairie: "From Illinois and Indiana came a later myth of all the people in the world at Howdeehow." It was planned that "at a given signal they would join in a shout." But when the signal was given, all the people from all the continents stood and listened, because they wanted to hear the great single shout. They all listened, "And the silence was beyond words." Finally the silence was broken by "a little old woman from Kalamazoo," who "was stone deaf." She "gave out a long slow wail over what she was missing." The single sound would have been the first word of the people as the people, the family of man. At it, they would have known they were one. But they became one by their silence, and they became one by the humanity of the stone-deaf woman who spoke for them. The first word was not Jove. It was a completely human word or beginning of a word—a shout, a noise made by one of the people—the old woman who represented them all. The first sound of birth is the cry.

Sandburg says: "This is the tale of the Howdeehow powpow, One of a thousand drolls the people tell of themselves" (2). The dictionary definition of "pow" is the sound of a blow or explosion. The people understand themselves through tall tales of how things came about. We listen to them and realize how they are "Grown in the soil of the mass of the people" (2). Without our participation in these tales we are nobody and by participating in them we are everybody. "The people know what the land knows" (2). We may ask: "Who shall speak for the people?" (24). And we may answer that the people speak for themselves, and we may listen and find ourselves as part of the people, because "The people is Everyman, everybody. Everybody is you and me and all others" (14).

Sandburg says: "And the people listen. As on the plain of Howdeehow they listen" (14). What is this word, "Howdeehow," one of the few words Sandburg coins, or perhaps coins? The people meet each other and they say "Howdee," and "how-de-do." It is prairie language, prairie speech. "Howdeehow" is a joke the people make on their own language, on the way they speak to themselves, and you either get it or you don't. If you don't get it, you likely never said, "Howdy" (how do you do; hello). The people have their own version of themselves, whether biblical or just something they say. In the poetic portraits of the people that follow Sandburg's descriptions of these original gatherings, each one of the people, in effect, says "Howdee" to us, and they proceed to introduce themselves through the expressions that Sandburg has listened to and recorded for the reader to hear.

It is necessary, for anyone to be anyone, to have a sense of origin. We know who we are because we each have an autobiography we carry with us in our personal memory. Without this sense of origin, of our childhood, we have no center to our persona. We are fragmented. We do not know who we are. We may think that to be something, we must be something we are not. This absence of self is not Sandburg's problem. To write as he does is to avoid anything that is "exclusive," to be willing to be who he is and where he is from. Sandburg never forgets his origin. This self-acknowledgement is what we can learn from his poetry. Everything Sandburg writes says who he is, and who we are. His poems are direct speech, as if he were engaged in documentary photography, making pictures as they happen, snapshots of the human. A poem in this sense literally is a gallery of pictures.

When reading Sandburg, as when reading Joyce, we are required to hear the words. And what we hear are topics or places in the memory. The syllables are echoes of what we have heard before but perhaps put aside in an effort not to have our language be so "Americanese." It is also possible and even probable that many readers have never heard what Sandburg heard, and have heard only what is formed in media-speech and the soulless language of administrators and managers. Nothing can be done for the reader who lacks a poetic ear. Sandburg's epic, in Joyce's words from *Finnegans Wake*, is "The last word in stolentelling!" (424.35), spoken from "the turrace of Babbel" (199.31).

Poetic Politics

On first looking into it, *The People, Yes* appears disorganized—just one thing after another. It is a glimpse of all that is really human. Sandburg said it was "Affirmative of swarming and brawling Democracy," but "Affirmative of 'democracy' it never mentions the word."[29] It appeared in the Great Depression, and was to counter the conditions of life and hardships the Depression brought, by an affirmation of the qualities of the American people and a verification of their ability to survive. As an epic poem it requires a hero, and the hero is the American people themselves. There is no central figure to be narrated except that of everybody, who can appear everywhere and who is both an individual and an embodiment of the universal of humanity. The first part of the poem is about the past, beginning with its myths of origin. The long middle part is a list of the present conditions of democratic life, and the last part is concerned with the future.

In this structure, the odyssey of the poem follows the principle of the Muses, to sing of what was, is, and is to come. The Muses can sing true and false songs, but true songs when they will. Sandburg's song is one of the true songs—not in any way false. Sandburg speaks the truth without devolving into sincerity, for he is always ironic. He is a master not only of metaphor but also of the ironic opposites in all human affairs. The course of

29. Niven, *Sandburg*, 504.

his poem is a comedy, in the sense that its outcome is positive, in the sense that the people persist. Sandburg presents human beings and the events that surround them both as they are and as how they should be. No theory guides the poem. As a poem it has the unique power to allow us to feel what democracy is and should be. As any novelist can tell more about the human psyche than any psychologist can, so poetic politics can tell more about democracy than any theory of political science can.

My aim is to course through some of the sections of *The People, Yes* in an effort to grasp the poem, to some extent, as a whole—and in this way to try to see its truth. This is my theme: Without the people, politics takes over all forms of human life. It becomes Leviathan; no hook can catch it. The people are the subject matter to which politics must connect. If the people are not there then politics will consume every aspect of human life. It will make every human action, all speech and thought, the servant of its standard, its shallowness. Politics is humorless, and humor is the life of the people. The mediocrity of the political is offset by the people, who base their life on the land where they are and on each other, on who they know each other to be. Only poetry can reach the people, tell us who they are—because poetry can understand their speech.

Politics is always simply administration. It is lifeless. The political always struggles with the poetical. The poet presents a world that is not made for doing business. Politics would have the people rely on it, but the people rely on themselves, on their own work, on the way they have learned to live in the world. Politics is in a constant task to convince the people to depend on it, on the mentality of the mass, the universal. The people are distinct from the political life of the mass. The people is a spirit of individuals, held together by common sense, by the real terms of human life. This sense of life that is in the people is why we can speak of "the people, yes," and not of "politics, yes." Politics is the activity of the abracadabra boys, who never know who they are. Thus politics gives them a purpose and a life. Politics erases all morality of the individual and replaces it with a "morality" of the mass. What is bad in politics is not the possibility of corruptions it can allow; it is the sincerity of imposing its standards of the mass as a morality on the people. The corrective to this imposition is the poetic politics of the people.

Although Sandburg's poem has a beginning, middle, and end, it is mostly middle, mostly the present. The middle is a great parade in which the human condition passes by the reader, in all the forms, all the

The Politics of *The People, Yes*

self-expressions of the people of which Sandburg can think—all of those he has stored in his memory for years. Except for the beginning and end, the numbered sections can be read in any order. The spectator at the parade can run along its route, back and forth, see it in any order, then find a vantage point and see it again. In this way, "We'll see what we'll see." Of the people, "The story goes on and on, happens, forgets to happen, goes out and meets itself coming in, puts on disguises and drops them" (32).

Once he got the idea, Sandburg wrote things down more or less as they came to him. As he says, of the unemployed in the Depression, marching around the country "they fall into a dusty disordered poetry" (101). The poetic disorder of the people is, in the end, what they are, and things are all right that way because that way, things remain alive and do not disappear into theoretical abstractions or the programs of political campaigns. "The people know what the land knows," namely, that things come and go and repeat themselves (4). The politician knows only the latest idea of progress and reorganization.

In the panhandle of Texas, a rider appears on the horizon. Riding all day, he arrives late, but not too late for supper (3). An old-timer living in the desert says that he has seen it rain and that he hopes it might rain sometime so his son could see it (4). In Knox County, Illinois, there is a barn of pine wood that has stood as a witness to sixty years' worth of farm work. Now it is nearly falling down, held up by some poles on the east side and by the pressure of the wind on the west (5). In Colorado, two men lie buried in the same grave. They shot it out over a piece of real estate, but they sleep now as neighbors (6).

Mr. Eastman, the inventor of the Kodak camera, who made millions, awoke one morning and carefully prepared to shoot himself, in his bathroom. There was nothing left for him to accomplish, so why wait? His suicide spared him having a second childhood (7). A father tells a son that, since life is hard, he must be like a rock, but it is good to be a fool every so often. He should tell no lies about himself and know that he can be different from other people, and solitude will let him have time for work that is his own (9). An Australian mounted infantryman, with a doctor's degree from the University of Heidelberg, who now teaches in a college in the West and who is a world traveler, once camped in front of the Great Sphinx in Egypt. One morning he asked the Sphinx to tell him something worth telling. The Sphinx, breaking its long silence, said: "Don't expect too much" (10).

The Philosophy of Literature

The teaching of the Sphinx is the teaching of the Stoic. You can get by if you don't expect too much. The people know this because they know that nothing really changes. Opposites are the North and South poles of life. From one thing comes another—its opposite. "The people, yes, out of what is their change from chaos to order and chaos again?" (58). The people look at things and they do not especially see progress, but they do see change. In this sense the people are innately philosophical. Although what changes remains the same, it is interesting to see what follows. "'It annoys me to die' said a philosopher. 'I should like to see what follows'" (58). There is a little Stoic in every philosopher.

It is best not to expect too much. "The ingenuity of the human mind and what passes the time of day for the millions who keep their serenity amid the relentless processes of wresting their provender from the clutch of tongs organized against them—this is always interesting and sometimes marvelous" (61). Ingenuity allows us to see the similar in the dissimilar, to see the coming together of opposites. Ingenuity makes us observers of the passing scene. It is what keeps the people going. They have seen it before, but it is always worth seeing again. The people never lose interest. They know that, if they do, there is nothing else for them. This life you got and you might as well make the best of it. Nothing much will change, but if it does, it is good to be there to see it.

This change through opposites is the natural order of things. Nothing can escape it. "The grass lives, goes to sleep, lives again, and has no name for it" (60). This change through opposites is rooted in time; it is the action time takes on things. "Time toils on translations of fire and rain into air, into thin air" (60). The four elements combine with each other: earth in which the grass lives, then fire and rain into air. So it is also in the order of the human world. "The poobahs rise and hold their poobah sway till their use is over and other poobahs hitherto unheard of step into their shoes and sit at the big tables and have their say-so till events order the gong for them" (66). Even those who think they own the world, do not. They are not indispensable.

One poobah is as good as another. They are interchangeable. No one is the master of time. Everyone has an opposite to take its place. In the same way, "the fathers can never arrange for the sons to be what the fathers were in the days that used to be" (66). The sons may replace the fathers but they cannot be made to be what the fathers were. And this cycle will happen to the sons, too. The sons succeed the fathers and then become fathers. Thus,

The Politics of *The People, Yes*

"both the people and the poobahs—life will not let them be" (66). The river of life is constant in its flow. "The same great river carries along its foam-flecks of poobahs and plain people" (66). Neither the great, who control the lives of the people, nor the people themselves, transcend the river of life and time. "A few stand, a few last longer than others while time and the rain, water and air and time have their way" (66). We, thinking we are observers, may ask, as Sandburg asks: "'Whither goest thou? whither and whither?'" (66). The poobah has no destination except to be the poobah.

The people have no aim but to be themselves. Although different from the poobah, whose only business is business, the people may answer: "Whither thou goest, I will go. Let my people be thy people." And the people speak their purpose in a language the poobah does not understand. The people's business is the people. They have seen the river and know what the river can do. For the people have come "From the four corners of the earth, from corners lashed in wind and bitten with rain and fire, from places where the winds begin" (1). The people are the soil out of which society comes and they, like nature itself, are nourished by the four elements. The people can always go back to what they are. That is what sustains them. They are of the land and the land is of them. The others, who live off the people, have no basis for self-reliance. They have no defense against time, but they do not know it. As Sandburg says in one of his *Smoke and Steel* poems, "Death Snips Proud Men": "Death is stronger than all the governments because the governments are men and men die and then death laughs: Now you see 'em, now you don't."[30]

"'The people is a myth, an abstraction.' And what myth would you put in place of the people?" (17). The people are the migratory harvest hands, the berry pickers, the metal polishers, the paint-sprayers who put the finish on cars, the riveters, the cowhands, the ex-convicts, the hotel bellhops, the union organizers, the ambulance crew, the meter readers, the fishing-boat crews. "The people is a lighted believer and hoper. . . . The birds of the air and the fish of the sea leave off where man begins" (22). The people have memory and what has happened today will happen tomorrow. Memory is what holds things together. It is the keystone in the arch. With it the arch is one piece. The people work and their work becomes what they are: "We'll see what we'll see. Time is a great teacher. Today me and tomorrow maybe you. This old anvil laughs at many broken hammers" (30).

---

30. Sandburg, *Complete Poems*, 177.

The Philosophy of Literature

The people do not expect too much. Memory holds time in the balance and prevents the illusion that the future will likely bring progress with it. Sandburg begins considering the question of the people and the future in the last sections of the poem. Since he is writing during the Depression, he is concerned with whether the people can survive it, and if the future of American society and economy is dependent on the people as America has been dependent on the people to build itself into a real nation. The people are the anvil, not the hammers; they are still surviving and will survive. The people know enough to hold on to the past as the key to the future: "As though yesterday is here today and tomorrow too will be yesterday and change on change is never hammered on the deep anvils of transition" (101). Sandburg reports the constant attempt to dominate the people—to use their work and their lives as nothing but a means for the manufacturers, the banks, and the railroads, the mines, the steel mills, the corporations—to make money. But the anvil of the people knows the art of persistence. The people have no choice except to go on from wherever they find themselves. "The people hold to the humdrum bidding of work and food" (107). They cannot be bought because they always hold to what they are.

It might be thought that this conception of the people is romantic. It must be admitted that, in a sense, it is romantic. But the romance of America is there; the evidence for it is in the language of the people. They speak for themselves. Who will speak for the people? The people will speak for the people. The poet only listens and preserves what the poet hears. Sandburg says: "The people will live on. . . . You can't laugh off their capacity to take it" (107). But as the people march on, with the fixed stars overhead, Sandburg asks, in the last line of his poem: "'Where to? what next?'" (107).

Where to? what next?

We now stand well into the twenty-first century, eighty years since Sandburg published his poem of the march of the people. In these decades, the conception of American society has changed. Two forces have taken shape. Technology has transformed America into an electronic world, and of late the doctrine of "political correctness" has pervaded every aspect of the American Dream, making it the American Nightmare. American society has become the technological society, as has a great deal of human society.

The philosophical sociologist Jacques Ellul is the first thinker to recognize acutely the principles of technological life. The fundamental motive of technological life is the search in every area of human activity for "efficient ordering," for the "one best means." Following Ellul, we may distinguish traditional society from technological society.[31] The historical dividing line between these two forms of society is the industrial revolution of the 1730s. In the Industrial Revolution, machines became means for production. Machines in this sense differ from tools. Tools are extensions of the human body that facilitate work. A machine, as different from a tool, has its own capability of motion once it is set in motion. The machine can go forward to accomplish an act of work with only some dependence on its operator. A tool taken out of the hands of the worker stands inert.

Traditional society depends upon the "technical operation" to accomplish work. The technical operation is accomplished by the use of tools and simple machines that require the constant effort of the worker or operator. Ways of accomplishing things evolve and alter through natural use. The mentality of technical operation is not progress; instead, it is tradition. Things are done the way they are done because they have always been done that way. These ways incorporate the wisdom of the ancestors that are characteristic of a given culture. The means by which work is accomplished are separate from how things are done in other areas of traditional society—in religious rites, artistic performance, social practices and customs.

Technological society depends upon the "technical phenomenon." For traditional society, technology is simply *techne*. With the advent of technological society, technology becomes not simply a way of doing things; it becomes a way of thinking about the nature of things. This way of thinking involves the constant posing of two questions: How can any way of doing things be improved? How can any way of doing things found successful in one area of human activity be transferred and employed in other areas? These are the questions necessary to the accomplishment of efficient ordering. Society is transformed by the use of machines as means of production, but this transformation is completed by a change in mentality. An immediate way to see this transformation is to note the constant presence of the survey. The worker is expected not only to perform the duties of a job but to assume the further duty of considering how what is being done can be improved and possibly expanded. The consumer cannot merely be a customer but is asked to improve the process itself. In universities and colleges

---

31. Ellul, *Technological Society*, 19–22. See also the discussion of technological desire in Verene, *Self-Knowledge*, 141–91.

the student is understood as a client, asked to fill out course questionnaires for the ever-present administrator.

These questionnaires are of a piece with those found on tables in restaurants, in hospitals at the point of the patient's discharge, in motel rooms, placed on the bureau for the guest, and in the follow-up contact from the car company, asking the buyer to rate the service. The suggestion box is everywhere. It is the phenomenon of the pragmatists' philosophical absolute of growth. The questionnaire, the survey, has little value in terms of its apparent aim of improvement. Its value is in reifying the idea of improvement itself. The individual is tied to the collective. Analogously, every advertisement, every television commercial, is about its particular product, but more importantly, it is about accustoming the recipient to the commonality, the naturalness of the commercial itself as a form of experience.

Technology is not only a means for transforming how work and production of goods is accomplished. It is a means of transforming the relationship we have to ourselves as humans. Technology, in the form of electronic devices, relieves us of the burden of thought and the burden of language. We need only look into the computer screen to experience something. We need no longer look at the world, at other people to whom we might speak, or at ourselves. At the computer we assume a meditative pose that precludes any possibility of meditation. Being *engagé*, nothing more is required or desired. Everything must be done through electronic media. Nothing need be done face to face. As in the modern, fully automated factory, the presence of the worker-operator is nearly incidental, so in modern business, human contact is not often needed. Nothing is real unless it can take electronic form. When it takes this form, then we can respond to it. It becomes real.

The individual is left speechless and valueless. The technological individual is valueless because there is no choice in regard to the one best means. Whatever can be done, will be done. As Ellul puts it: "Modern society is, in fact, conducted on the basis of purely technical considerations. But when men found themselves going counter to the human factor, they reintroduced—in an absurd way—all manner of moral theories related to the rights of man, the League of Nations, liberty, justice. None of that has any more importance than the ruffled sunshade of McCormick's first reaper. When these moral flourishes overly encumber technical progress, they are discarded—more or less speedily, with more or less ceremony, but with determination nonetheless. This is the state we are in today."[32] Where everywhere there is no real individuality, there is everywhere talk of individuality and the rights of the individual. All values are relative to technological advance. Technological advance is not teleological; it aims at no purpose other than itself. Thus, for any problem caused by technology, the solution is a technological solution.

The technological "individual," stripped of all value, has the submerged sensation of the apocalypse, of something that cannot be fully grasped, coming up behind. It is the feeling that something has been left out in the formation of the technological society. The sights and experiences of being before the *Wunderkammer* of technology are too good to be true. The technological person suffers from the presence of his own shadow. The problem is this: there is no technique of self-knowledge; there is no technique of what the human being is. This lack of such a technique is what is meant when we say technology is dehumanizing. In the technological society the individual is left with techniques of self-help, which are programs for living more efficiently. The technological person is the functionary—the administrator of his or her own existence.

Left valueless, the individual is left speechless. What is there to say? Language is reduced to nothing at all, to the shorthand speech, the electronic grunts and exclamations of "texting." They are the scratchings on the cave wall. To call such exchanges "texting" is a vacant wish, for no text is involved at all. A text is language with content, a formulation of thought put into words that requires meditation and reflection to seek out its meaning. The idea of a text bears no resemblance to "texting." With the speech of morals made irrelevant to human action, such speech becomes a decoration, at most to grace the pursuit of the one best means in any area of social life. All that is left is political speech, and the announcing of opinions on "social media," which bears no sense of human society whatsoever. "Social media" is in no sense social.

It is no surprise, then, that the speech of moral correctness, once rooted in the norms of traditional society, is replaced in technological society with the speech of political correctness. The relationship between individuals and of the individual to the social order at large is seen wholly in political terms. Human relationships are negotiations. Eccentricity is not allowed because whatever shape it takes may be a matter of discomfort to others. The categorical imperative, which asserts to act always such that your

---

32. Ibid., 74.

actions could become a universal law, is slightly modified to advocate to act such that your actions can become an instance of social justice. Justice, that value of all values that can be held onto by an individual as transcendent of any current state of opinion, is reformed as "social justice." There is no justice. There is only the standard that the prevailing social mentality holds to be the standard. This standard is ever shifting, just as politically correct terminology is ever shifting, because it is based in opinion, not in reason. What is one day acceptable speech is not the next, having been replaced or amended by even more correct and "more inclusive" speech.

The many are convinced they have found a standard, only to find another to succeed it, losing their memory of the one before it. The many, caught up in political correctness, constantly cross the river Lethe. They advocate tolerance but are intolerant of any deviation from their tolerance. In place of the American Dream, the language of political correctness substitutes diversity. Diversity is the word used for tolerance in politically correct speech. But only certain forms of diversity are allowed. Diversity does not allow for the diversity of exceptions, for the truly eccentric. The technological person lives within the prison-house of politically correct language. As the technological world is a *huis clos*, and we find ourselves within technique's filing cabinet, so politically correct speech and the thought that resides in it is a *huis clos*, and we find ourselves tongue-tied within it, unable to allow words to be themselves.

If we look within this world, a world Sandburg missed seeing, by just a few years, where are Sandburg's People? Where to? what next? turned out to be what Sartre saw: no exit; what Beckett saw in *Waiting for Godot*, and what Eliot saw in the *Wasteland*. Is it possible still to find the people in among the technological persons, in among their administrated, electronic lives? Does the Land still exist? Is there still a fine smoke, in which people move? Is the "howdeehow" speech of the people somewhere to be found? Is the anvil of the people still there, if we know where to look for it?

Sandburg's faith in the future and the people, that he shared with Whitman, is a stand against what the philosophy of technology tells us of the state of contemporary society. In *The People, Yes* we encounter a version of how the business of modern life has transformed the means of production, human work, and social economics. But beneath these forces Sandburg has uncovered the human society of the people. It is the authority of the people that, Sandburg proposes, will keep us safe and keep the family of man alive. If we listen, we will be able to locate the presence of the people

The Politics of *The People, Yes*

through their speech. They are our only hope. They are our dream out of time. They are our contact with everyman. They are our understanding of self-reliance in the face of the future.

Are the people still with us? There are still people who work for a living—the window-washers, freight hostlers, sweepers, warehouse clerks, sackers, cooks, bakers, snowplow drivers, road workers. There is work that is just work, that is not simply done at a computer. But the lives of the non-technological workers are fully involved in electronic space and time. Sandburg called television the "idiot box" but he never saw a personal computer or an electronic phone.

For the people to survive in the technological society, they must be able to form themselves as individuals who are at the same time citizens. The self, to be a self, must be able to think. To think means to have an "inside." The way the people speak issues forth from this inside. Without it, speech is a flow of personal opinions and reactions, a kind of mental epidermis. The constant possibilities of technological communication make everyone involved in it a journalist, that is, the putting of the moment into words that shortly becomes as stale as yesterday's newscast. Journalism is the thought-form of technological life. Thought and the use of language need go no farther than that of the journalist. The image of the journalist as talker and thinker is everywhere. It is the model of the fully prepared, modern person. Constantly to be in touch with others in electronic exchange is not to have friends; it is to have contacts and to mistake having contacts for friendship and conversation.

Technology is not about the past or the future; it is an eternal present in which there is constant change without purpose, only a constant modification and alteration of itself, such that the individual becomes deeper and deeper in these developments that substitute for self-development. When the people pass out of themselves into the constant gaze of the technical they lose the basis to be themselves. They lose the land and they lose language. They lose the human inside. In the technological universe there is no poetry and there is no irony.

Missing too are imagination and memory. Information is only facts and instructions. It is the opposite of the speculative sense of experience. There is just information—information about oneself, information about anything and everything. Information is neutral, and because it is neutral it is a world in which anything can be said with equal importance. The technologically engaged person seeks recognition. This quest for recognition that accompanies the general quest for certainty in all matters that the technological society offers, takes the form of putting forth "my opinion." It is a constant cry in the dark.

The people no longer have a language of their own. So many of the people have no language, at all. They have no experience at all that is not derived from the media. Work is no longer a way of life; it is something one does and attempts to get out of, whenever possible. There is little contact with the land. The family of man has been replaced by the doctrine of "globalization." It is not "politically correct" to use the term "political correctness" because it makes it appear to be a doctrine of society, when it is intended as the form of society itself. It is not intended to be a prescription for correct speech, but to be speech itself.

When read today, what Sandburg's speech of the people can do is cause us to remember the manifestation of the human before it became consumed by the electronic universe. It cannot take us into the future but it can preserve the past. Poetry acts against time because time eats all things. Poetry takes us out of time and into memory. It is our memory that allows us to stand apart from the rational madness that is the technological universe, and that consumes wisdom. The Republic of Letters remains our only place of refuge. All else has gone with the winds of change. In the technological society that is today, Sandburg's voice, and the voice of the poet generally, is heard only by the few who still listen.

4

The Phenomenology of *The Ship of Fools*

The Fool as a Human Type

References to the fool as a human type can be found throughout philosophical and literary works. The *Urtext* for all understandings of the fool and folly is Sebastian Brant's *Das Narren Schyff*, published in Basel in 1494, written in Medieval German. In three years it was translated into Latin by Brant's pupil, Jacob Locher, and by 1548, translations appeared in Low German, French, English, Flemish, and Dutch. With Brant's *Narrenschiff*, German literature entered into the world of European letters.

I wish in this chapter to connect Brant's *Narrenschiff* and Hegel's *Phänomenologie des Geistes*. My approach is one of philosophy *and* literature. This approach, as part of the field of the philosophy of literature, is characterized by raising a given issue and inquiring into what may be learned by viewing it from both a philosophical and a literary perspective. These perspectives stand to each other in a dialectical relationship. They are approached as two different ways of thinking, considered such that one supplements and, to an extent, completes the other. Brant's *Ship of Fools* portrays forms of thought, speech, and action that are illusions that divert those caught up in them from finding the right path to truth. Hegel's *Phenomenology of Spirit* is a sequence of stages in which consciousness deludes itself, on each stage, into holding that it has achieved the unity of subject and object, only to discover that the unity is in fact an illusion and that the true stage of "absolute knowing" is yet out of reach.

The idea of folly and the presence of the fool as a figure in society was of particular interest in the late medieval world and into the Renaissance. Erasmus, in *Moriae Encomium, The Praise of Folly*, calls attention to the connection of folly to happiness, as reported by Horace. Horace says: "Once at Argos there was a man of some rank, who used to fancy that he was listening to wonderful tragic actors, while he sat happy and applauded in the empty theatre—a man who would correctly perform all other duties of life, a most worthy neighbour, an amiable host, kind to his wife, one that could excuse his slaves, and not get frantic if the seal of a flask were broken, one that could avoid a precipice or an open well."[1]

His deliberate self-delusion appeared to his friends as a kind of madness, but it was in fact just another way of approaching the world. The theater is a version of the world in which anything can happen, depending upon the imagination of the playwright. The noble Greek at Argos simply imagined his own plays. They were not hallucinations of a mind gone mad. He inverts the traditional order of the theater. The stage became the audience to his internal stage. Horace says: "This man was cured by his kinsmen's help and care, but when with strong hellebore he had driven out the malady and its bile, and had come to himself again, he cried: 'By Pollux! [*pol*] you have killed me, my friends, not saved me; for thus you have robbed me of a pleasure and taken away perforce the most pleasing wandering of my mind.'"[2] His friends thought him mad and cured him by means of *helleboros*, the powder of the poisonous root used in the ancient world to cure mental disorders.

Erasmus observes all of the human scene as in the *theatrum mundi*. He says: "Now what else is the whole life of mortals but a sort of comedy, in which the various actors, disguised by various costumes and masks, walk on and play each one his part, until the manager waves them off the stage?"[3] Horace's Greek in the empty theater has double vision. He can see the world as others see it; thus he has the ability to act in the agreeable way he does with his friends and wife and household. But he has another reference point in his imaginations in the empty theater. He has his own theater of the world within the theater of the world that he recognizes as society. He

---

1. Horace, *Epistles* 2.2.128–40.
2. Ibid. See also Erasmus, *Praise of Folly*, 52.
3. Erasmus, *Praise of Folly*, 37.

The Phenomenology of *The Ship of Fools*

has the second sight of the fool, which corrects the ordinary vision through which others see themselves and the world.

Diogenes the Cynic was a master of the logic of the fool, of fool-business. Menippus, in his *Sale of Diogenes*, relates that, having been captured, Diogenes was put up for sale as a slave. He was asked what he could do. "He replied, 'Govern men.' And he told the crier to give notice in case anybody wanted to purchase a master for himself."[4] "Asked why people give to beggars but not to philosophers, he said: 'Because they think they may one day be lame or blind, but they never expect to become philosophers.'"[5] "At a feast certain people kept throwing all the bones to him as they would have done to a dog [*cynic*: "dog"]. Thereupon he played a dog's trick and drenched them [urinated on them]."[6] Once Diogenes "was asking alms of a bad-tempered man, who said, 'Yes, if you can persuade me.' 'If I could have persuaded you,' said Diogenes, 'I would have persuaded you to hang yourself.'"[7] The postmodern philosophers, with all the cleverness they attempt, cannot touch the humor of Diogenes. Diogenes truly knows how to see the other side of things.

Rabelais describes an academic debate in which Panurge represented his master, Pantagruel, in a dispute with a great English scholar, Thaumaste (whose name is a play on Greek *thauma*: "wonder"). Panurge is a (Greek) *pantomimos*, an actor, mimic. That he is true to his name emerges quickly, when we learn that the debate will be conducted wholly in signs. Thaumaste approaches the physically huge Pantagruel and claims to quote Plato: "How true it is, as Plato, prince of philosophers, says, that if the image of wisdom and learning is a physical matter, visible to human eyes, it excites the whole world with admiration."[8] We soon learn that the debate will be conducted in a bodily manner, a series of epistemic gestures. Since Thaumaste has come from England to debate Pantagruel, Pantagruel spends the night reviewing great texts that he may need for the debate. But then Panurge tells Pantagruel he wishes to debate the Englishman on his behalf. Instead of study, Panurge spent the night drinking and playing games with the servants.

---

4. Diogenes Laertius, *Lives* 6.29.
5. Ibid. 6.56.
6. Ibid. 6.46.
7. Ibid. 6.59.
8. Rabelais, *Gargantua and Pantagruel*, 190.

When the debate is to begin, Panurge steps forward. Rabelais says: "But note, please, that Panurge had hung a handsome tassel of red, white, green, and blue silk at the end of his long codpiece, and inside it he had stuffed a fat, juicy orange."[9] The debate begins with Thaumaste and Panurge exchanging complicated hand signals. The first sign Panurge makes is to stick "his thumb into his nose, keeping the other four fingers extended in a row straight out from the tip of his nose."[10] The hand gestures of Thaumaste are the presentation of abstract forms, whereas those of Panurge are bodily. He waves his long codpiece at Thaumaste. Thaumaste rejoins by puffing out "his cheeks like a bagpipe musician, blowing as hard as if he were inflating a pigs bladder." In response, "Panurge stuck one finger of his left hand right up his ass, sucking in air with his mouth, as if eating oysters in the shell or inhaling soup."[11]

Thaumaste "pulled out a dagger, holding it with the point facing down." To this abstract gesture, Panurge "grabbed his great codpiece and shook it against his breeches as hard as he could. Then he joined his hands like a comb and put them on top of his head, sticking out his tongue as far as he could and rolling his eyes like a dying goat." Thaumaste counters this full body pose with some weak hand signals and puts his fist against his forehead. Then to end the whole exchange, "Panurge put his forefingers on each side of his mouth, pulling back as hard as he could and showing all his teeth. His thumbs drew his lower eyelids as far down as they would go, making an exceedingly ugly face, or so it seemed to everyone watching." Thaumaste has no choice but to admit defeat, saying: "Gentlemen, now I can truly speak the biblical words: *Et ecce plus quam Solomon hic*, And here is one who is greater than Solomon."[12] Panurge the mime has translated his master's learning into body language and won the day.

Panurge is a fool-mime. He has defeated the Englishman by the fool's *folie*. The fool's scepter has been transformed by Panurge into his great codpiece, the double of himself with which he threatens his opponent. When he puts his finger in his nose he makes a beak, the symbol of the cock, the fowl, the classic symbol of the fool. Thaumaste makes a weak counter by puffing out his cheeks as if inflating a pig's bladder. The fool is associated with the Latin word *follis*: "a leather bag, bellows, windbag," also "puffed-out

9. Ibid., 194.
10. Ibid.
11. Ibid., 196.
12. Ibid., 197.

The Phenomenology of *The Ship of Fools*

cheeks." Thaumaste's attempt at his own fool-sign loses the contest of puffing and blowing when Panurge turns all of himself into an inverted bellows, sucking in air. Panurge makes a coxcomb with his hands on his head—also the sign of the fool. Imitating a goat, he makes Thaumaste the butt of the joke.

In a last-ditch effort, Thaumaste tries to make a rooster's beak by putting his fist up against his forehead, but fails to make a beak. Panurge tops this by turning his whole face into the exaggerated smile of the clown with drooping eyelids. Panurge's command of the wisdom of the fool defeats the sincerity of the Englishman. Anything the Englishman signs is ironized. Panurge sees right through it. Thaumaste is so overcome that, in a sincere declamation, he compares Panurge to Solomon.

The fool as a human type did not always act alone. The fool's art suggested the possibility of a society of fools that would be the inversion of society. A society of fools, called the Babinian Republic, was formed in Poland in 1568. It functioned as a shadow government, with a duplicate of the Polish constitution, and created a complete set of offices, held by fools. Admission to the Babinian Republic was gained if someone did something sufficiently foolish. If the invitation to join was not accepted, the person was hounded until he did accept. "He was then given a license with a large seal and an office appropriate to his folly. If, for example, he had talked knowingly of things he did not understand, he was made an archbishop." The society became a double for all the branches of government as well as the church. "Finally the King of Poland, Sigismund August II, asked whether the Babinian Republic also had a king and was told that as long as he lived the society would not dream of electing another."[13]

The fool as a looking-glass, in which we can see ourselves as others see us, becomes a literary theme, often with philosophical overtones. There are the wise fools of Shakespeare, especially Falstaff and Lear's fool, and the antics of Don Quixote. In *Candide* Voltaire employs the figure of Doctor Pangloss to turn into folly the Leibnizian doctrine that "everything is for the best in this world." Swift's Laputian professors in *Gulliver's Travels* occupy a place in the annals of folly; they carry with them huge bundles of the objects known to them, as the means of displaying their knowledge to one another.[14] By the eighteenth century the devices of folly have become

---

13. Quoted in Willeford, *The Fool*, 226.
14. Swift, *Writings*, 158–59.

instruments of criticism. The fool has begun to lose his status of a benign figure.

By the beginning of the nineteenth century the fool figure becomes exhausted and the fool becomes a causality of natural selection. A text of the period states that the fool's "exercises are commonly divided into four parts, eating and drinking, sleeping and laughing: for these are his chief loves; a bauble, and a bell, coxcomb, and a pied coat: he was begotten in unhappiness, born to no goodness, lives but in beastliness, and dies but in forgetfulness. In sum, he is the shame of nature, the trouble of wit, the charge of charity, and the loss of liberality."[15] The fool in his rooster-suit of feathers and beak, symbolizing the power to herald the first light of dawn, in which everything is suddenly seen differently, is now an aberration of nature, an unproductive member of society. The fool with the double of his scepter no longer possesses the power of self-vision. He is at best a distraction and at worst a social danger. In the late 1960s, in Vancouver, British Columbia, the position of "town fool" was created, supported by a grant from Canada Council. But he roamed the streets "like a living fossil, looked at with amusement or anger but drained of any socio-cultural and metaphysical function."[16]

The medieval fool was understood as *deviatus*, thus something negative, but he was also referred to by such words as *stultus, stolidus, idiotus, insapiens, lunaticus*, and *melancholicus* (a term also used since Aristotle to denote the philosophical temperament). As Anton C. Zijderveld points out, for the medieval mind and society the fool "could not be denominated by one single epithet, as Rational Man would do: 'mental patient.' It is also obvious that all these colourful names were but variations of one theme: the fool as a looking-glass image of the 'normal' human being."[17] The modern rational man simply sees the fool as lacking rationality and thus a person who needs to be cured or controlled. The fool, then, in principle as well as in fact, has no positive value for the aims of modern bourgeois life. Having no positive way to understand human folly, the most that folly can be is a subject of comic entertainment.

In the film *Animal Crackers* (1930), Groucho Marx's brother says to him: "He thinks I look alike." Groucho replies: "Well, if you do, it's a tough break for both of you." In another place Groucho divides himself in two,

---

15. Quoted in Swain, *Fools*, 185.
16. Zijderveld, *Reality in a Looking-Glass*, 162.
17. Ibid., 35.

The Phenomenology of *The Ship of Fools*

and the two Grouchos interact. The fool is the master of the double. The fact that the fool incites laughter makes him an agent of the human. When we can laugh we know we are human. In the onset of clinical mental illness, the sense of humor is the first quality of the person to disappear. The mentally ill always take themselves and their problems and anxieties completely seriously. They do not have the ability to step back from their situation, whatever it may be, and find humor about themselves. Missing from the world of the mentally ill is the joke.

The inversion of events and self-doubling that characterize the power of the fool, and which the fool brings to every situation, reminds us of the arbitrariness of the structure of our ordinary life. Zijderveld describes a twentieth-century domestic fool, Peppi, a member of the household of Zijderveld's parents-in-law in Vienna. Throughout his life, Peppi would intersperse his sentences and gestures with a repetitive *bitte-danke, danke-bitte* (please-thanks, thanks-please).[18] If irritated by a question, he would rattle this phrase off several times as answer. He would also interrupt conversations with the same series of expressions. Given the polite repetition of these words in German conversation, Peppi was holding up to it a linguistic mirror. His interruption means: Why say one thing rather than another? What is said might just as well be said in the opposite. We might just as well back into a room as enter it straightforwardly. We might just as well thank someone before we request something. And the reverse.

It is all just words, anyway. Peppi was in no sense mentally ill. He insisted on doubling everything up. As a fool, his folly was likely monotonous and not especially instructive, but his ordering of the world was not without interest and was entirely harmless. Philosophically, the words and actions of the fool raise the question of the logic of inversion, of the topsy-turvy as a principle of experience and the development of human consciousness.

The Inverted World

Hegel wrote the *Phänomenologie des Geistes* (1807) while he held his first university teaching position at Jena. In his foreword to the English translation, John Findlay says that, in the Jena lecture rooms, Hegel was seized by a divine imparting of knowledge, "an afflatus perhaps unique in philosophical history, which affected not only his ideas but his style, and which makes one at times only sure that he is saying something immeasurably

18. Ibid., 166–67.

The Philosophy of Literature

profound and important, but not exactly what it is. (I am in this position, despite help, regarding the two intelligible worlds in the section on Force and Understanding.) To comment on Hegel fully would therefore require the same sort of psychological and metapsychological treatment that has long been practised on an essentially rapt man like Shakespeare or on such a Gallic genius as Rimbaud or Mallarmé."[19]

Harold Bloom, in his study of the literary sublime and its relation to the production of knowledge by genius, *The Daemon Knows*, says: "Ultimately, the philosophical daemonic will end in the preface to Georg Hegel's *Phenomenology of Spirit*, where we must practice a Dionysiac whirl in order to see the ultimate vision the sublime yet may promise. All authentic shamans, like so many dervishes, are devoted to exuberant whirling. The daemon, who divides and distributes, knows through whirling what stasis never brings."[20] Bloom's reference is to the famous passage in Hegel's preface to the *Phenomenology* that portrays his vision of philosophical knowledge: "The True is thus the bacchanalian revel at which no one is sober, but because each by so separating itself from the whirl is immediately absorbed by it, it is just as much a state of transparent, unbroken calm."[21]

Hegel then states the point of his metaphor: "Judged in the court of this movement, the single shapes of Spirit do not persist any more than determinate thoughts do, but they are as much positive and necessary moments, as they are negative and evanescent. In the *whole* of the movement, seen as a state of repose, what distinguishes itself therein, and gives itself particular existence, is preserved as something that *recollects* itself, whose existence is self-knowledge, and whose self-knowledge is just as immediate existence."[22]

Hegel's philosophical *Bildungsroman* of spirit (*Geist*), coming to know itself through the stages in which human consciousness comes to know that the object it wishes to grasp (*begriefen*) is in fact itself, is a drama showing the True to be the Whole. The key term of the dialectical movement of these stages that form the whole is the untranslatable German verb, *aufheben*. *Aufheben* as a philosophical term is an ironic holding together of two senses of things—cancelling and preserving. It has the double meaning of speaking against what it wishes to speak for. Hegel's dialectic has often been

---

19. Hegel, *Phenomenology*, xiii.
20. Bloom, *Daemon*, 155.
21. Hegel, *Phänomenologie*, 39. My translation.
22. Hegel, *Phenomenology*, 27–28.

The Phenomenology of *The Ship of Fools*

thought to be a process of synthesis, in which one stage of consciousness is taken up in the next, in an ever-enlarging production of the whole. But this interpretation forgets from the start that the whole is what truly exists as the one actual individual.

The dialectic of Hegel's phenomenology or "science of the experience of consciousness" is a process of recollection (*Erinnerung*). The *Phenomenology of Spirit* is a memory theater. What we remember is no longer actually present; it has been outlived, cancelled. But it is preserved in memory. It is thus *aufgehoben*. Self-knowledge is an act of memory in which each thing remembered is detached, but once detached, falls straightway back into the ever-developing whole of consciousness that is memory in the sense of recollection, that is, in the sense of a progressive grasping of things in a causal order. Recollection, then, is a kind of reasoning.

The section of the *Phenomenology* in which Hegel introduces his principle of the inverted world is that on "Force and Understanding: Appearance and the Supersensible World." It comes just at the end of the general stage of "Consciousness" from which spirit passes into "Self-Consciousness." By means of the inverted world, consciousness leaves its attachment to knowing the object as something external to itself and realizes that it has the freedom to take itself as its own object. Consciousness realizes that it has a self and that the self is. How this transition comes about is presented in some of the most complicated passages in Hegel's corpus, as Findlay has noted.

The phenomenon of inversion that Hegel makes explicit in the final stage of the development of consciousness of "Force and Understanding" is operative from the very first moment of the *Phenomenology*. Consciousness, uncertain of the reality of its object, asserts that in the least it is certain of what appears to the senses as a particular. Consciousness is certain of the object as a "this." "This" is a "here" and "now." Consciousness, then, is certain of the sensed object as *my* object, as being *mine*. It is what I know without qualification. The *Phenomenology* opens with a pun on *mein*—the possessive adjective "mine"—and *meinen*—the verb "to opine," the nominative of which is *Meinung*, as in *meine Meinung*, "my opinion." Here is the Platonic world of the ongoing flux of sense perceptions, mirrored by the instability of opinion. As soon as consciousness attempts to affirm the reality of the particular as certain, the word for the greatest sense of particularity is identical with the word for the greatest sense of universality. "This," used to designate the sheer particular, is the same word that is used to designate anything and everything.

The Philosophy of Literature

There is nothing in our experience as conscious beings that cannot be called a "this." The same can be said of "here" and "now." Any place that is, is a "here," and any moment that is, is a "now." Particulars cannot be known, because to know something is to be able to state its difference from another thing. To call something a "this" is to call it what anything and all things can be called. The particular is inverted to the universal. The particular can only be thought as in some sense a universal. Consciousness has in the most minimal way realized that to know its object, the object must be grasped as particular and universal at once. The search for the certainty of the sensible particular as the basis of knowledge is a fool's errand. It is an illusion.

Animals, not burdened by the presence of language, demonstrate their own wisdom by eating up particulars. Particulars can be eaten, digested, enjoyed, but they cannot be thought. From this first scene of the oscillation between the poles of particular and universal, consciousness goes forth to attempt to overcome this phenomenal *aporia*. Motivating this going forth is Aristotle's observation that all human beings desire to know. Animals, not having this desire, roam the world, content to live with and through particulars. Their world is never subject to an internal inversion. But the human animal cannot escape from the phenomenon of inversion of its world. Only the achievement of absolute knowing will offer relief.

In Hegel's inverted world we may find the phenomenological basis for the fool's metaphysics of reversal. The source of Hegel's term, *verkehrte Welt*, is, without question, Ludwig Tieck's play with the same name. Eight years before Hegel published his *Phenomenology*, Tieck published *Die verkehrte Welt*. It was the basis of a considerable controversy. Tieck's publisher, C. F. Nicolai, refused to publish it. Tieck wrote the play in 1797; the first version of it appeared in *Bambocciaden* (1799), a miscellany edited by A. F. Berhnardi (Italian: *bambocciata, bambocceria*, childishness, silly action). The characters in Tieck's play—for example, the main character, Scaramuccio—have a connection with *commedia dell'arte*, but the theme of *Verkehrung* is deep in German consciousness and German literature.

Karl Rosenkranz, in *Geschichte der deutschen Poesie im Mittelalter* (History of German poetry in the Middle Ages) relates the theme of *verkehrte Welt* to that of the *Narrenschiff* (ship of fools) and the *Totentanz* (dance of death). The Grimm brothers' *Deutsches Wörterbuch* cites Brant's *Narrenschiff* as a source for the verb *verkehren*.[23] Michel Foucault, in his *Histoire de la Folie*, says that the ships of fools did exist and that the insane

---

23. For a full discussion of these points see Verene, *Hegel's Recollection*, 50–55.

The Phenomenology of *The Ship of Fools*

cargo of fools was sent from town to town. Foucault says, of the fool: "He is the Passenger *par excellence*: that is, the prisoner of the passage. And the land he will come to is unknown—as is, once he disembarks, the land from which he comes."[24] Are we not the prisoner of the passage Hegel presents in his "science of the experience of consciousness" that takes us from the natural standpoint on the object to an inversion of this standpoint to the subject—ourselves? Hegel says: "When natural consciousness entrusts itself straightway to Science, it makes an attempt, induced by it knows not what, to walk on its head too, just this once . . . relatively to immediate self-consciousness it [*Wissenschaft*] presents itself in an inverted posture [*als ein Verkehrtes*]."[25]

The Dance of Death involves *Verkehrung*, in that it puts life in the mirror of its opposite. The Dance of Death unsettles our ordinary grasp on things. Death dances with everyone. In 1401, in the first work of German literature, *Der Ackermann aus Böhmen* (*The Plowman from Bohemia*), by Johannes von Saaz, is: "the earth and all that therein is are built upon transience. In our day they have become unsettled, for all things have been reversed [*alle ding haben sich verkeret*], the last has become the first, the first has become the last, what was below has risen above and what was above has fallen below. The greater part of people has turned wrong to right."[26]

Tieck's play, which was never performed in his lifetime, and even now has rarely been performed, begins upside down, with an Epilogue, and concludes with a Prologue. An audience is placed on stage, watching a play, with this play visible to both audiences—the one in the play and the one attending the play. A member of the onstage audience suddenly changes places with one of the actors. Many reversals or *Verkehrungen* occur. One of the fictive spectators cries out: "What if we were fiction too?" At the end of the play, Prologue enters, as if a character in the play. But the stage is empty, with all the actors having gone behind the curtain. In the final speech of the play, Grünhelm says: "Ha! Here was a whole Prologue directed at me, namely one of the chief personages in the play, and yet he remained completely unaware of my presence, and yet I'm the only person here! This is a marvel that deserves to be investigated by the philosophers."[27]

---

24. Foucault, *Madness and Civilization*, 11.
25. Hegel, *Phenomenology*, 15.
26. Johannes von Saaz, *Plowman*, 103–4.
27. Tieck, *Land of Upside Down*, 121.

Hegel investigated it and concluded that the key to self-knowledge is appearance of the self to the self, through the breakdown of the ability of consciousness to assure itself of the truth of its knowledge of the object. Consciousness, in its attempt to know the thing-in-itself, realizes it can know for certain only the appearance of the object. But once we can know only the appearance of the object, we have lost any standard against which to evaluate what appears. In the world of appearances, one is as true as another. We find ourselves wholly in the sensible world, separate from the supersensible world of the thing-in-itself. To attempt to solve this problem, consciousness abandons the thing-in-itself as a substance and replaces it with the thing as a play of forces. The play of forces is imminent in the world of appearances, whereas the thing-in-itself as substantial ground of the appearance is transcendent, supersensible. The play of forces makes it possible to conceive the world of appearance as law-like, as having a total structure. All laws are unified in the concept of "universal attraction," which asserts "that *everything has a constant difference in relation to other things*."[28]

Law is present in a "two-fold manner" because it is the same as force—force is what differentiates itself from itself, yet is drawn back into itself. Hegel gives the examples of such laws of force as those of electricity, which acts as positive and negative, and gravity, which accounts for up and down motion. Hegel says: "In the play of Forces this law showed itself to be precisely this absolute transition and pure change; the selfsame, viz. Force *splits* into an antithesis which at first appears to be an independent difference, but which in fact proves *to be none*."[29] The law of forces simply shows how what acts in one direction can as well act in the other. The original version of the supersensible world of the thing-in-itself was in some sense a copy of the perceived world. But when its laws are expressed as forces that split into differences that are not really differences but just selfsame alternations, then the Understanding (*Verstand*) enters the inverted world. Hegel says: "According, then, to the law of this inverted world, what is *like* in the first world is *unlike* to itself, and what is *unlike* in the first world is equally *unlike to itself*, or it becomes *like itself*."[30]

The Understanding is incapable of thinking beyond this movement between two poles. We take the pole of positive electricity and the other is negative; we take the negative pole and the other is equally the negative

---

28. Hegel, *Phenomenology*, 91.
29. Ibid., 96.
30. Ibid., 97.

of it. Electricity is *both* positive and negative, both and neither. Since the Understanding thinks by placing all things into a classificatory scheme, it enters the swoon of the inverted world. It is unable to fix the difference in a sustaining element. It is simply a dialectic of back and forth, the opposite of an opposite. There can be no dialectical movement forward, toward a further grasp of the object, when there is a perfect standoff of two opposites. One is the inversion of the other, yet they are somehow the same thing. The Understanding cannot comprehend something that is the opposite of itself since there is no way to categorize the difference.

It is here, in the final pages of his presentation of "Force and Understanding," that Hegel provides a dialectical version of Descartes's *cogito*. In his *Meditations on First Philosophy*, Descartes introduces his famous assertion of his self-existence by a three-stage progression of hypothetical doubt. He asks the reader to consider, first, that there are grounds to doubt at any time what the senses are presenting to the mind. We are aware that we are sometimes deceived in terms of what we are seeing or hearing, thus we have no assurance that at any given moment what we perceive is not a deception. Second, our awareness of our bodily state, our internal perception, may be fallible. We have had the experience of dreaming we were in one state or another, only to awake and realize we were only dreaming. At any given moment we have no proof we are not dreaming.

Third, when we come to a conclusion by ratiocination derived wholly apart from sense perception, we must consider the possibility that there is an anti-god, an "evil genius" that could cause my conclusion to be false, even though I can find no reason to think so. The evil genius then becomes a principle, for Descartes, to doubt all that is in his senses and in his thought. Reason as precisely as I may, I could in principle still be deceived. Descartes's *malin genie* is Hegel's *verkehrte Welt*.

Descartes's solution is suddenly to declare that "*I am, I exist*, is necessarily true whenever it is put forward by me or conceived in my mind."[31] With this discovery Descartes has acquired his Archimedean point from which to lift the world. He has discovered a single certainty, from which he claims to deduce the great truths that first philosophy seeks. Descartes is a master of the theater—and of the mask that the philosopher requires to pass hidden in society. In his private notebooks, Descartes says: "Just as comedians are warned not to allow shame to appear on their brows, and thus put on a mask: so I, about to step upon the theater of the world, where

---

31. Descartes, *Writings*, 2:17.

I have so far been a spectator, come forward in a mask."[32] His notebook entry is of a piece with his motto, *Bene qui Latuit, bene Vixit*—"He who is well hidden, lives well." In the *Discourse on Method* Descartes says that during the nine years he spent roaming the world, he attempted "to be a spectator rather than an actor in all the comedies that are played out there."[33] Descartes in mask, in the *theatrum mundi*, passes back and forth from the persona of actor to spectator. In the *Discourse* we look into his room at Ulm, where he is seated at his *pôele* as if on a stage set, while he addresses his audience, inviting them to think along with him.

In the final paragraph of "Force and Understanding" Hegel says that consciousness, facing the inversion of its world, "experiences only itself. Raised above perception, consciousness exhibits itself closed in a unity with the supersensible world through the moderating term of appearance." The two extremes—that of the pure, inner world of the known object and the pure, inner world of the knowing subject—coincide. Thus "the vision of the undifferentiated selfsame being, which repels itself from itself, posits itself as an inner being containing different moments, but for which equally these moments are immediately *not* different—*self-consciousness*." The stage is set. The audience is ready, having gone through the moments of inversion, as described in Tieck's play. The stage-curtain is thus suddenly drawn away and the "I" is revealed, gazing into the "inner." ("Dieser Vorhang ist also vor dem Innern weggezogen, und das Schauen des Innern in das Innere vorhanden.")[34] Hegel uses the term *Vorhang* specifically, meaning a stage-curtain.

Here is Descartes's *cogito*, standing before us, the product of the hypothetical doubt of the world-inversion of the *malin genie*. Hegel says: "It is manifest that behind the so-called curtain that is supposed to conceal the inner world, there is nothing to be seen unless we go behind it ourselves, as much in order that we may see, as that there may be something there which can be seen."[35] With this going behind the scene, Hegel says, the Understanding as our way of knowing vanishes. We take up the project of self-knowledge. We have lost the certainty of the external object but gained self-certainty.

32. Descartes, *Cogitationes*, 213. My translation.
33. Descartes, *Writings*, 1:125.
34. Hegel, *Phenomenology*, 103.
35. Ibid.

The Phenomenology of *The Ship of Fools*

Hegel has replaced Descartes's conception of first philosophy based on deductive reasoning with first philosophy based on dialectical reasoning. We find ourselves in the theater of the world and our guide is not the theoretical possibility of the *malin genie* but the actual dialectic daemon of the fool, who is our necessary companion, who guides us toward the doubleness of truth—that all truth is partially error and all error is partially truth. The philosopher who has come through the labyrinth of the inverted world has learned to walk upside down, because the principle of inversion is the key to the method of dialectic that will govern each stage of the *Phenomenology* as its reader progresses toward absolute knowing.

The Ship of Fools

In *A Midsummer Night's Dream*, Robin, the tailor, says to Oberon, King of Fairies: "Shall we their fond pageant see? Lord, what fools these mortals be!"[36] We may ask: What are the follies of the pageant of the human race? We can turn first for an answer to the pre-Shakespearean compilation of 112 types of fools occupying the cabins on Sebastian Brant's *Narrenschiff*, on its way to the land of Narragonia. The mortal fools emerging onto the deck of Brant's ship are engaged in follies that detract them from the path they should be finding for themselves toward Christian salvation. Their follies cause them to stray from the self-knowledge they need to live properly. Thus the Prologue begins with: "All lands in Holy Writ abound / And works to save the soul are found." Then continues: "Who know but folly, to their shame, / Yet will not own to folly's name."[37] The one-hundred and twelfth chapter points to Socrates as the example of a wise man. Socrates is "A good, wise man of prudence rare, / As one can find scarce anywhere."

Brant sees Socrates as the Virgilian *Vir bonus*, and urges the reader to read this verse. The true wisdom of the good man is to be found there. Brant concludes: "May God place that in every hand, / I hope, Sebastianus Brant" (112). In the *Eclogues* of Ausonius is "De Viro Bono" that is part of the corpus of Virgiliana, or at least associated with it. The eclogue concludes: "Thus he [*vir bonus*] goes into all his words and acts, and turning all

---

36. Shakespeare, *Complete Works*, 413. act 3, scene 2, lines 114–15.

37. Brant, *Ship of Fools*, 57. Hereinafter citations to Brant's work are in the text by their chapter numbers.

The Philosophy of Literature

over when evening is come, he condemns the bad and gives the palm and the prize to the good."[38]

Brant's work has woodcuts depicting the type of fool for each chapter. The woodcuts are associated with Albrecht Dürer in style; he or his school are their likely source. Dürer met Brant in Antwerp in 1520, when he sketched his portrait.[39] Brant's work is not original. He notes that his work is *gesamlet*, that is, collected.[40] The metaphor of the ship is also not original. The idea of a ship of fools was widespread from Holland to Austria, and was the subject of orations, several works, and a sermon. The portraits of the fools are likely a reflection of the practice of the Swabian *fliegende Blätter*. Flysheets showing types of fools were circulated, with the title: *Der ist ein Narr* (This is a fool).

Brant's work is an encyclopedia of folly and illusion. The chapters can be read in any order. Brant says: "With caution everyone should look / To see if he's in this my book" (1). Indeed, Brant includes himself in the next to last chapter, "Apology of the Poet." He confesses: "Of folly I was never free. / I've joined the fool's fraternity." He says that, try as he has, his "fool's cap will not come off" (111). But he hopes to improve over time. The method Brant advocates to overcome folly is to appeal to God and simply to do better. It is just the method of trying to be a good Christian.

In Ecclesiastes we find: "So I turned to consider wisdom and madness and folly.... then I saw that wisdom excels folly as light excels darkness. The wise have eyes in their head, but fools walk in darkness" (2:12–14). Brant's metaphor of the ship echoes not only the passages on folly in Ecclesiastes but the Christian tradition of the church as the ship of St. Peter. Jesus embarks on a ship with his disciples (Matt 8:23–27, Mark 4:36–41). Jesus preached from Peter's boat (Luke 5:3). The ship of Christian faith is carried over rough seas to its port in heaven. Brant's ship is the inverse of this heavenly ship. It is a recall of those who have strayed from the Christian faith and the good Christian life. Brant's ship holds those who have wasted or are in the process of wasting their substance in folly of all types. Their watery souls are on a journey without purpose, moving about aimlessly in life.

Brant's poetic text is done in rhymed couplets, expertly preserved in the English translation by Edwin Zeydel. These rhyming couplets hold the reader's attention and affect memory. Furthermore, by being a constant

---

38. Ausonius, *Eclogues* 3.24–26.
39. Brant, *Ship of Fools*, 20.
40. Ibid., 15.

repetition of feminine rhymes they convey a kind of lightness that offsets their ponderous message.[41] Brant has a sense of irony, These fool-stances in the woodcuts and texts make us not take ourselves too seriously. We see ourselves as others likely see us. We see that we, along with humanity generally, cannot avoid folly. Folly seems to come with the fall of man. We look in Brant's book and think: Yes, that's right. Everyone is human. It has a stronger moral message than does Erasmus's *Praise of Folly* but it is not an indictment of humanity. It is a comedy in the sense that all can be well if it ends well. And we learn from Brant's book that all will be well if we absorb its message.

We will have set ourselves on the path to Socratic wisdom, which is endorsed in the final chapter. Socrates admits that he does not know, and so can accept the Delphic precept of the pursuit of self-knowledge, which is to find the answer to the question of what it means to be a human being. If we admit that we are caught up in one kind of folly or another, we can accept the Christian precept of the *vir bonus*.

Brant's Christian optimism is contrary to the view in the rest of the passage from Ecclesiastes quoted above, which says: "Yet I perceived that the same fate befalls all of them [both the wise and the foolish]. Then I said to myself, 'What happens to the fool will happen to me also; then have I been so very wise?' And I said to myself that this also is vanity. For there is no enduring remembrance of the wise or of fools, seeing that in the days to come all will have been long forgotten" (2:14–16).

Thus Brant's book is the mirror of humanity: "For fools a mirror shall it be, where each his counterfeit may see." This mirror will show us the truth about ourselves: "His proper value each would know, the glass of fools the truth may show." If we find our reflection, then we know we are not yet wise: "Who sees his image on the page may learn to deem himself no sage." The purpose of the book is to have "The world's whole course in one brief look." Brant says: "One vessel would be far too small to carry all the fools I know." Indeed there were works written later, influenced by Brant, that added many more fools to the ship. Brant says there is no one who is without folly in some sense: "Both men and women, all mankind their image in this glass will find."[42]

Brant has produced for his readers a *speculum stultorum*. The forms of foolishness that appear range from "Of Useless Books" (1) (those who

---

41. See the rhymes in the original edition, Brant, *Das Narren Schyff* (1494).
42. These lines are from the Prologue; see Brant, *Ship of Fools*, 58–61.

involve themselves in collecting books in order to glorify themselves, but do not understand the books they have) to "Of Useless Studying" (27) (those who have not learned the proper things). "Thus money spent to train and school has often gone to rear a fool," to "Innovations" (4) (over-attachment to fashions and the new), to "Taking Offense at Fools" (40) (those who ridicule fools or do not heed them, thus quickly becoming fools themselves), to "Blowing into Ears" (101) (those who pass on what others say), to "Of Not Taking a Joke" (68) (the folly of arguing with fools).

In addition to these follies are ones we might expect, those concerning envy, hatred, complacency, anger, pride, adultery, bad manners, ingratitude, gambling, gluttony, pursuit of riches, contempt of holy writ, making noise in church, sowing discord, blasphemy, and so on. There are some esoteric follies, such as "Useless Hunting" (74) (spending too much time at it) and "Experience of All Lands" (66) (being interested only in other places—our modern infatuation with "globalization"). We do not live in Brant's world, but his forms of folly are mostly still here although they go by other names. They are here, if we only look.

Erasmus, the Renaissance satirist, is in contrast to Brant, the scholasticist. Erasmus met Brant in 1514 and admired him greatly.[43] He was familiar with the *Narrenschiff* before 1509. His metaphor is not the ship but the theater of the world. Society is a stage-play and Erasmus is its satirist. Erasmus asks what Ecclesiastes means "when he writes 'Vanity of vanities, all is vanity,' what else do you think he means but that, just as I have told you, human life is nothing but a sport of Folly."[44] If all is vanity, with each person playing nothing but a role of one kind of self-importance or another, then the stage-play of life is meaningless. Even to be the spectator of this play is itself a role. Does the *Praise of Folly* contain a further doctrine? The key passage in Erasmus's satire is that the fool is the practitioner of "true prudence."[45] The fool does not act on the basis of books or philosophies. The wisdom of the fool is to accept the conditions of life and act on them by the power to see through any situation to its opposite: the fool's method of inversion.

The fool takes events not as fixed but as subject to being seen from the opposite perspective, by having a nature other than they seem to have. The fool is not afraid to act, and acts out of his own innocence. In so doing

---

43. Brant, *Ship of Fools*, 6–7.
44. Erasmus, *Praise of Folly*, 106.
45. Ibid., 36.

The Phenomenology of *The Ship of Fools*

the fool prevails because he is not overcome by events. In this way the fool shows it is possible to act in any situation. There is no set of events not subject to interpretation in terms of folly and none in which the fool cannot act. When others stand still before a condition, the fool surprises us with the totally unexpected response. The fool accomplishes this response without any theory. The fool just acts out of his own nature.

As ignorance is a necessary presupposition of the pursuit of wisdom, folly is a recurring presupposition of our pursuit of virtuous action. The fool is not in possession of any cardinal virtues, but the fool is basically good and honest. The practice of particular virtues in the conscious pursuit of the best life requires correct reason, as Aristotle says, yet reason that allows for the presence of folly allows us to be human, to act in a fully human way. The fool shows us what it means to act directly from what we are. Brant and Erasmus both ask us to see ourselves with the aid of their pictures of human folly. The human comedy is the basis of this self-instruction. We discover who we are by seeing ourselves in their mirror. Folly, our constant companion, with us because we are human, guides us toward happiness, but it is not happiness itself.

The positive doctrine of happiness to be found in Erasmus is the happiness of accepting the folly in which we all participate. Erasmus's favorite word, *festivus* ("festive," "cheerful," "companionable"), describes the quality that characterizes the good life. We approach life like the fool, on our own terms, but these terms are offset by a sense of decorum. In our sense of decorum we depart from the action of the fool. Decorum is beyond the fool's reach. Without decorum, life would be simply a comedy of errors, a silly sequence of events signifying nothing. Erasmus's sense of *festivus* has a resonance with Ecclesiastes: "There is nothing better for mortals than to eat and drink, and find enjoyment in their toil" (2:25); "I know that there is nothing better for them than to be happy and enjoy themselves as long as they live" (3:12). These sentiments do not appear in Brant's sense of prudence.

If we regard Erasmus's book as a kind of sequel to Brant's, and historically it is, we can see they are joined by a commitment to prudence. They both speak to the individual. They are not social reformers. Good individuals make a good society. Their concern is with the individual, how the individual is best to exist. Brant regards wisdom as a counter to folly. There is nothing positive in what the fool does. Folly interferes with our proper cultivation of the soul. Wisdom in Brant's conception is practical wisdom (*prudentia*), not theoretical wisdom. Erasmus, the humanist, gives no instruction in the salvation of our souls comparable to the moralism of Brant. Yet Erasmus is a proponent of the truth of the original Christian faith. In the *Praise of Folly* Erasmus is concerned with how the individual might be festive in the face of the foibles of social life and its institutions. Thus being able to see the folly in human affairs is a necessary wisdom; it allows us to see things as they are. To see things as they are is the very basis of prudent action. To see the irony in a situation is the master key to human prudence.

In his 1515 letter to the theologian Maarten van Dorp, explaining his book, Erasmus reveals that prudence has been his guide to write it. Erasmus says: "You can see that everywhere I've always been careful to avoid anything which could be offensive. But those whose ears are open only to propositions, conclusions and corollaries pay no heed to that."[46] Brant, in introducing the folly of the presumptuousness of pride, says that to act in an attempt to achieve notoriety will always fail in the end, and we will see: "That he has been misled by pride / And but on rainbows has relied" (92). Both the poet and the philosopher must chart a careful course in advancing their images and ideas. They will not be understood by those who can think only in propositions or, in an opposite manner, may themselves be overcome by a quest for notoriety.

Absolute Wisdom

In concluding his transcendental analytic, the heart of his *Critique of Pure Reason*, and before entering into his transcendental dialectic, Kant presents the one poetic passage in his book. It describes the pure Understanding as the "land of truth." Kant has happily put everything that pertains to the Understanding in order. He can now pause briefly to celebrate this achievement. He says: "We have now not merely explored the territory of pure understanding, and carefully surveyed every part of it, but have also measured its extent, and assigned everything its rightful place. This domain is an island, enclosed by nature itself within unalterable limits. It is the land of truth—enchanting name—surrounded by a wide and stormy ocean, the native home of illusion, where many a fogbank and many a swiftly melting iceberg give the deceptive appearance of farther shores, deluding the adventurous seafarer ever anew with empty hopes, and engaging him

---

46. Erasmus, "Letter to van Dorp," 158–59.

The Phenomenology of *The Ship of Fools*

in enterprises which he can never abandon and yet is unable to carry to completion."[47]

Kant's efforts in formulating the elements of the understanding have led him to the kingdom of Prester John, in epistemological form. If we have made the journey with Kant, we now have arrived finally at a certain place in which all is certain. We are at a version of Descartes's Archimedean point, a place to stand. Moreover, we have followed Descartes's advice, as Kant's last sentence in this passage glosses Descartes's warning to avoid fictitious narratives, because those who are taken with them "are liable to fall into the excesses of the Knights-errant in our tales of chivalry, and to conceive plans beyond their powers."[48] To seek the transcendental realm of Ideas, where only dialectic and speculative reason reign, is to find ourselves in the *Abenteuer* of deluded seafarers, or the *extravagance* of paladins, tilting at windmills, engaging in the fictions of thought, for, Kant says, the dialectic of pure reason is a "logic of illusion."

What lies outside this land of analytic truth is the world of the thing in itself—the noumena. If we dwell only on the island of the Understanding, we can know the world of appearances perfectly: the phenomena. Fear of error, timidity of soul, will keep us at home, with what we can know with certainty. To allow thought to sail into the metaphysics of Ideas is to end in the shipwrecks of paralogisms, antinomies, and impossibilities of the ontological, cosmological, and physico-theological proofs for God's existence. We can spare ourselves this fate if we stick to the schematizing of the pure concepts of the Understanding, even though: "This schematism of our understanding, in its application to appearances and their mere form, is an art concealed in the depths of the human soul, whose real modes of activity nature is hardly ever likely to allow us to discover, and to have open to our gaze."[49]

The schematism is almost a mysterious stranger who commands *eine verborgene Kunst*—a hidden art with which we have to deal. But dealing with the art of this stranger gives us the certainty of the categories necessary for ordering appearance. Dialectic governs the far-off land of illusion, where one thing can simply lead us to another, including its opposite. In dialectic we lose the security of the phenomenal object and find the object to be part of ourselves. Folly requires dialectic, in which truth and error meet

---

47. Kant, *Critique of Pure Reason*, 257.
48. Descartes, *Writings*, 1:114.
49. Kant, *Critique of Pure Reason*, 183.

each other. In the land of the Understanding folly is impossible, unless our confinement on its island is itself a folly. Could this land of truth perhaps in fact be part of Narragonia—a land whose residents are rationally mad?

In his preface to the first edition of his book, Kant says: "Our age is, in especial degree, the age of criticism [*Kritik*], and to criticism everything must submit."[50] Critical thinking is a folly Brant has left out, unless it might fall under pride or useless studying. Criticism keeps thought constantly engaged with the matter-in-hand, the *Sache selbst* that Hegel describes in his phenomenology of *das geistige Tierreich* or "spiritual menagerie," in which everyone is academically busy with expounding and justifying a project, while feigning interest in all the projects of others. The mentality of the Understanding fails to realize that its distinction between the thing as it appears and the thing in itself is a distinction thought makes for itself. It is a dialectical relationship within thought.

To forget this distinction is analogous to failing to realize that the island is an island because of what is not the island—the surrounding sea and the manifestation of its presence. Criticism, like argument itself, presupposes a narrative in which the points it makes have meaning. Narrative is an act of memory in which the interrelations of the past, present, and future come alive. Wisdom depends on not forgetting the doubleness that dominates experience—that as the past gives way to the future, anything gives way to and presupposes its opposite.

The conclusion of Hegel's *Phenomenology of Spirit* is the achievement by *Geist* of "absolute knowing." Each stage of the *Phenomenology* is an illusion that the conditions of absolute knowing, of wisdom, have been met, only to find that this stage is superseded by another, making it a "highway of despair." It is a ship of fools. The answer to the ship of fools is the theater of memory. The final paragraph of Hegel's book is the realization that all is memory. He says that this succession of stages of spirit (*Geister*) is a gallery of images (*Galerie von Bildern*), now held in memory by consciousness.[51] These are a master set of topics from which we can draw and apply to any situation in which we find ourselves, for any such situation will fit into one or more of the structures of consciousness that have been elicited in the succession of stages of the *Phenomenology*.

Hegel's book, in the end, is a book of prudence, for knowing in advance that a situation in which we find ourselves, for example, has the logic

---

50. Ibid., 9n.
51. Hegel, *Phenomenology*, 492.

The Phenomenology of *The Ship of Fools*

of the stage of master-servant, which lets us know how to act within it. Or knowing that what is before us is an instance of the "beautiful soul" lets us know what comes next. Or, encountering a situation of an unbridgeable gap between two alternatives that mimics that of the unhappy consciousness, we know how to think it through. Or, confronting a bogus theory of human psychology, we can respond to it in terms of Hegel's analysis of phrenology. Absolute knowing is to know how to employ the forms of consciousness as we move through life. All great works of philosophy are instructions in the philosophical life, in what the philosopher needs to know to live in the *polis*.

The *Phenomenology of Spirit*, like the *Ship of Fools*, is an instruction for those who can comprehend it, an instruction in confronting illusion. When undergoing its various stages of self-development, Hegel says, consciousness forgets that its previous stages have produced only the illusion of wisdom, of absolute knowing. Thus consciousness continually forgets itself and continually must begin *von vorne an*—must begin all over again. It must always begin anew. Wisdom requires that we respond to things as they really are. Wisdom is not the faculty of attempting to remake the world. It is the faculty of living well within experience as it actually is.

In the final paragraph, Hegel employs "recollection" (*Erinnerung*) in four senses to remind the reader of what the *Phenomenology* is.[52] In the first moment, spirit attempts to realize what it itself really is: "Since its completion consists in fully knowing what *it is*, its substance, this knowing is its *going into itself* in which it abandons its existence and gives its shape over to recollection." Having gazed at the gallery of images that spirit has formed of itself, it wishes to know what itself is as the knower of these images.

Spirit realizes that these images exist in its memory, its power to recollect them. Its existence is comprised of this total recollection, this hall of memory. Spirit is now in a state of selfsame immediacy "as if all that preceded was lost and it had learned nothing from the experience of the earlier spirits [stages of its knowing]. But the *re-collection [Er-Innerung]* has preserved this and is the inner being, and, in fact, higher form of substance." Spirit now realizes that these images are images of itself; they are in fact the forms of its inner life, its inside.

Next spirit realizes that these images that are the forms of its inner life are not simply forms of its subjectivity, they are the forms of human

---

52. Ibid., 492–93. The passages quoted here and to the end of the chapter are from the final paragraph of Hegel's text, with the translation slightly modified.

existence, of the human self itself. This realization of the subjective-objectivity of the images is the penultimate step to absolute knowing. "The *goal*, Absolute Knowing, or Spirit knowing itself as Spirit has for its path the recollection of Spirits as they are to themselves and accomplish the organization of their realm."

The recognition of the succession of images in this sense is to recognize their existence as history. It remains to recognize them both as history and as science [*Wissenschaft*]. "Their preservation, regarded from the side of their free existence appearing in the form of contingency, is history; but regarded from the side of their conceptually grasped organization, it is the *science of the coming into appearance of knowing*; both together—conceptually grasped history—comprise the recollection and the Calvary of absolute spirit."

As history, the images have a contingent order of one-after-the-other. This contingent sense of temporality must be transformed into a necessary sequence, of a knowledge *per causas* governed by the principle of *Aufheben*. Dialectical order is the real order of time in which things could not be otherwise. It is the time of autobiographical knowledge in which what has happened is recollected as a sequence that is not otherwise, nor ever could have been otherwise. Absolute knowing is to have "two thinks at a time," to think the contingent as necessary. This double thinking allows us to think history philosophically. Reason is both in the world and in the self; each is the completion of the other. Neither can substitute for the other.

Absolute knowing, then, is to grasp things as they truly are by inverting one side into the other. It is to be able freely to pass from history to philosophy and from philosophy to history. Neither is what it is without the other. Yet there is no form of thought that synthesizes these two into one. They are always a "twone." The Calvary of spirit is that the dialectic of consciousness is never terminated. Its life is its movement. Once we know how to think this opposition we possess absolute wisdom. We can move within the whole, which is the True, with the ease of the wise man of whom Brant speaks.

Philosophy conceived as absolute knowing is our defense against forgetting. Forgetting takes us immediately back into the illusions of the stages of the *Phenomenology*, into its forms of folly, into the bacchanalian revel as it is taking place. Absolute knowing places us at the point where it is grasped as a scene of unbroken calm. The attainment of wisdom is the attainment of peace. We can move about the world without the need

The Phenomenology of *The Ship of Fools*

for the categorical imperative, equipped to let prudence be our guide. The imperative, in its abstraction, can never tell us what to do. But absolute recollection can, because we know that what is now has been before and will be again. Hegel's system is a circle, and as he says, a circle of circles. It is a circle because time is a circle and time is the life of the self and the life of humanity that is inseparable from it.

The *Narrenshiff* and the *Phänomenologie des Geistes*, read together, are two sides of a coin. This double reading lets us think in both a literary manner and a philosophical manner at once. One need not be resolved into the other. From between them, Folly emerges and speaks its piece, and as we listen we may begin to see ourselves in their two mirrors. We see the double of ourselves.

Bibliography

Aquinas, Thomas. *Commentary on the Metaphysics of Aristotle*. Translated by John P. Rowan. 2 vols. Chicago: Regnery, 1961.
Aristotle. *The Complete Works of Aristotle*. Edited by Jonathan Barnes. 2 vols. Princeton: Princeton University Press, 1984.
———. *Nicomachean Ethics*. Translated by Robert C. Bartlett and Susan D. Collins. Chicago: University of Chicago Press, 2011.
Atherton, James S. *The Books at the Wake: A Study of Literary Allusions in James Joyce's Finnegans Wake*. Carbondale: Southern Illinois University Press, 2009.
Augustine. *The City of God Against the Pagans*. Translated by William M. Green. Cambridge: Harvard University Press, 2003.
Ausonius. *Eclogues*. In *Ausonius*, translated by Hugh G. Evelyn White. 2 vols. Cambridge: Harvard University Press, 2002.
Austin, J. L. *How to Do Things with Words*. Cambridge: Harvard University Press, 1962.
Bacon, Francis. "Of Vicissitude of Things." In *The Major Works*, edited by Brian Vickers, 451–54. New York: Oxford University Press, 2002.
———. *The Works of Francis Bacon*. Edited by James Spedding, Robert Leslie Ellis and Douglas Denon Heath. 4 vols. New York: Garrett, 1968.
Beckett, Samuel. "Dante. . . Bruno. Vico. . Joyce." In *Our Exagmination Round His Factification for Incamination of Work in Progress*, 3–22. New York: New Directions, 1972.
Berkeley, George. *Three Dialogues between Hylas and Philonous*. Edited by Colin M. Turbayne. Indianapolis: Bobbs Merrill, 1954.
Bloom, Harold. *The Daemon Knows: Literary Greatness and the American Sublime*. New York: Spiegel and Grau, 2015.
———. *The Western Canon: The Books and School of the Ages*. New York: Harcourt Brace, 1994.
Borges, Jorge Luis. *Collected Fictions*. Translated by Andrew Hurley. New York: Penguin, 1998.
———. *El inmortal*. In *El Aleph, Obras completes*, 7–26. Buenos Aries: Emecé Editores, 1957.
———. *The Immortal*. In *Collected Fictions*, translated by Andrew Hurley, 183–95. New York: Penguin, 1998.
———. *This Craft of Verse*. Edited by Calin-Andrei Mihailescu. Cambridge: Harvard University Press, 2000.
———. *Selected Non-Fictions*. Edited by Eliot Weinberger. New York: Penguin, 1999.

Bibliography

Brant, Sebastian. *Das Narren Schyff*. Edited by Manfred Lemmer. Tübingen: Niemeyer, 1968.

———. *The Ship of Fools*. Translated by Edwin H. Zeydel. New York: Dover, 1962.

Bruni, Leonardo. "The Study of Literature." In *Humanist Educational Treatises*, edited by Craig W. Kallendorf, 92–125. Cambridge: Harvard University Press, 2002.

Bruno, Giordano. *Cause, Principle and Unity*. Translated by Robert de Lucca. Cambridge: Cambridge University Press, 1998.

———. *The Expulsion of the Triumphant Beast*. Translated by Arthur D. Imerti. Lincoln: University of Nebraska Press, 1964.

———. *On the Infinite Universe and Worlds*. In Dorothea Waley Singer, *Giordano Bruno: His Life and Thought*, 225–378. New York: Schuman, 1950.

Cassirer, Ernst. *An Essay on Man: An Introduction to a Philosophy of Human Culture*. New Haven: Yale University Press, 1944.

———. *Language and Myth*. Translated by Susanne K. Langer. New York: Dover, 1953.

———. *The Philosophy of Symbolic Forms*. Vol. 4, *The Metaphysics of Symbolic Forms*. Translated by John Michael Krois. Edited by John Michael Krois and Donald Phillip Verene. New Haven: Yale University Press, 1996.

Cicero. *De oratore*. Translated by E. W. Sutton. Cambridge: Harvard University Press, 2001.

Collingwood, R. G. *An Essay on Philosophical Method*. Oxford: Clarendon, 1962.

Column, Mary and Padraic. *Our Friend James Joyce*. Garden City, NY: Doubleday, 1958.

Curran, C. P. *James Joyce Remembered*. London: Oxford University Press, 1968.

Dante. *The Divine Comedy: Inferno, Purgatorio, Paradiso*. Translated by Charles S. Singleton. Princeton: Princeton University Press, 1977.

DeArmey, Michael H., and James A. Good. *The St. Louis Hegelians*. 3 vols. Bristol, UK: Thoemmes, 2001.

Descartes, René. *Cogitationes privatae*. In *Oeuvres de Descartes*, vol. 10, 213–48, edited by C. Adam and P. Tannery. Paris: Vrin, 1996.

———. *The Philosophical Writings of Descartes*. Translated by John Cottingham, Robert Stoothoff, and Dugald Murdoch. 2 vols. New York: Cambridge University Press, 1984.

Diogenes Laertius. *Lives of Eminent Philosophers*. Translated by R. D. Hicks. Cambridge: Harvard University Press, 2000.

Ellmann, Richard. *James Joyce*. Rev. ed. New York: Oxford University Press, 1982.

Ellul, Jacques. *The Technological Society*. Translated by John Wilkinson. New York: Knopf, 1964.

Erasmus, Desiderius. "Letter to Maarten van Dorp." In *Praise of Folly*, translated by Betty Radice, 135–72. New York: Penguin, 1971.

———. *The Praise of Folly*. Translated by Hoyt Hopewell Hudson. Princeton: Princeton University Press, 1974.

Faulkner, William. *Requiem for a Nun*. New York: Vintage, 2012.

Foucault, Michel. *Madness and Civilization: A History of Insanity in the Age of Reason*. Translated by Richard Howard. New York: Vintage, 1973.

Frankfort, Henri et al. *The Intellectual Adventure of Ancient Man: An Essay on Speculative Thought in the Ancient Near East*. Chicago: University of Chicago Press, 1977.

Gillet, Louis. *Claybook for James Joyce*. Translated by Georges Markow-Totevy. London: Abelard-Schuman, 1958.

Bibliography

Glasheen, Adaline. *Third Census of "Finnegans Wake": An Index of the Characters and Their Roles*. Berkeley: University of California Press, 1977.
Goethe, Johann Wolfgang von. *Goethe's Faust*. Translated by Walter Kaufmann. New York: Random House, 1990.
Grassi, Ernesto, and Maristella Lorch. *Folly and Insanity in Renaissance Literature*. Binghamton, NY: Medieval and Renaissance Texts and Studies, 1986.
Guicciardini, Francesco. *Ricordi*. Milan: Rizzoli, 1977.
Hegel, G.W. F. *Phänomenologie des Geistes*. Edited by Johannes Hoffmeister. Hamburg: Meiner, 1952.
———. *Phenomenology of Spirit*. Translated by A. V. Miller. Oxford: Clarendon, 1977.
———. *Werke*. 20 vols. Frankfurt am Main: Suhrkamp, 1986.
Hesiod. *Theogony*. Translated by Glenn W. Most. Cambridge: Harvard University Press, 2006.
Homer. *Homeric Hymns, Homeric Apocrypha, Lives of Homer*. Translated by Martin L. West. Cambridge: Harvard University Press, 2003.
———. *The Odyssey*. Translated by Robert Fagles. New York: Penguin, 1996.
"Homer." In *The Oxford Classical Dictionary*, edited by N. G. L. Hammond and H. H. Scullard, 524–26. 2d ed. Oxford: Clarendon, 1979.
Horace. *Ars Poetica*. Translated by H. Rushton Fairclough. Cambridge: Harvard University Press, 1999.
———. *Epistles*. Translated by H. Rushton Fairclough. Cambridge: Harvard University Press, 1999.
The I Ching or Book of Changes. Translated by Richard Wilhelm and Cary F. Baynes. Princeton: Princeton University Press, 1997.
Joyce, James. *The Critical Writings of James Joyce*. Edited by Ellsworth Mason and Richard Ellmann. New York: Viking, 1959.
———. *Finnegans Wake*. London: Faber and Faber, 1939.
———. *Finnegans Wake*. Edited by Danis Rose and John O'Hanlon. Cornwall, England: Houyhnhnm Press, 2010.
———. *Letters of James Joyce*. Edited by Stuart Gilbert. New York: Viking, 1957.
———. *A Portrait of the Artist as a Young Man*. Edited by Seamus Deane. New York: Penguin, 1993.
———. *Selected Letters of James Joyce*. Edited by Richard Ellmann. New York: Viking, 1992.
———. *Stephen Hero*. Edited by Theodore Spencer. New York: New Directions, 1944.
———. *Ulysses*. Edited by Hans Walter Gabler. New York: Vintage, 1986.
Kant, Immanuel. *Critique of Pure Reason*. Translated by Norman Kemp Smith. London: Macmillan, 1958.
Longinus. *On the Sublime*. Translated by Donald Russell. Cambridge: Harvard University Press, 1995.
Machiavelli, Niccolò. *Machiavelli: The Chief Works and Others*. Translated by Allan Gilbert. 3 vols. Durham: Duke University Press, 1989.
McHugh, Roland. *Annotations to Finnegans Wake*. Rev. ed. Baltimore: Johns Hopkins University Press, 1991.
MacLeish, Archibald. "Ars Poetica." In *The Oxford Book of American Poetry*, edited by David Lehman, 385–86. New York: Oxford University Press, 2006.
Malinowski, Bronislaw. *Magic, Science and Religion*. Garden City, NY: Doubleday Anchor, 1948.

Bibliography

Mercanton, Jacques. "The Hours of James Joyce." In *Portraits of the Artist in Exile: Recollections of James Joyce by Europeans*, edited by Willard Potts, 205–52. New York: Harcourt Brace Jovanovich, 1986.

Nietzsche, Friedrich. *On the Genealogy of Morals*. Translated by Walter Kaufmann. New York: Random House Vintage, 1989.

Niven, Penelope. *Carl Sandburg: A Biography*. New York: Scribner's, 1991.

Plato. *Complete Works*. Edited by John M. Cooper. Indianapolis: Hackett, 1997.

———. *The Republic of Plato*. Translated by Allan Bloom. 2d ed. New York: Basic Books, 1991.

Plutarch. *Moralia*. Translated by Frank Cole Babbitt et al. 16 vols. Cambridge: Harvard University Press, 2000.

Quintilian. *Institutio oratoria*. Translated by Donald A. Russell. 5 vols. Cambridge: Harvard University Press, 2001.

Rabelais, François. *Gargantua and Pantagruel*. Translated by Burton Raffel. New York: Norton, 1990.

Rousseau, Jean-Jacques. *The First and Second Discourses*. Translated by Roger D. and Judith R. Masters. New York: St. Martin's, 1964.

Royce, Josiah. *The World and the Individual: First Series, The Four Historical Conceptions of Being*. New York: Macmillan, 1899.

Sandburg, Carl. *Always the Young Strangers*. New York: Harcourt Brace, 1953.

———. *The Complete Poems of Carl Sandburg*. Revised and Expanded Edition. New York: Harcourt Brace Jovanovich, 1970.

———. *The People, Yes*. New York: Harcourt Brace, 1964.

———. *Remembrance Rock*. New York: Harcourt Brace Jovanovich, 1948.

Santayana, George. *Three Philosophical Poets*. In vol. 6 of *The Works of George Santayana*, 1–142. New York: Scribner's, 1936.

Shakespeare, William. *The Complete Works*. Edited by Stanley Wells and Gary Taylor. 2d ed. Oxford: Clarendon, 2005.

Spengler, Oswald. *Der Untergang des Abendlandes: Umrisse einer Morphologie Der Weltgeschichte*. 2 vols. Munich: Beck, 1923.

Sproul, Barbara C. *Primal Myths*. San Francisco: Harper, 1991.

Straumann, Heinrich. "Last Meeting with Joyce." In *A James Joyce Yearbook*, edited by Maria Jolas, 105–15. Paris: Transition, 1949.

Swain, Barbara. *Fools and Folly During the Middle Ages and the Renaissance*. New York: Columbia University Press, 1932.

Swift, Jonathan. *The Writings of Jonathan Swift*. Edited by Robert A. Greenberg and William B. Piper. New York: Norton, 1973.

Tieck, Ludwig. *The Land of Upside Down*. Translated by Oscar Mandel. London: Associated University Presses, 1978.

Tindall, William York. *A Reader's Guide to Finnegans Wake*. Syracuse: Syracuse University Press, 1996.

Verene, Donald Phillip. *Hegel's Recollection: A Study of Images in the Phenomenology of Spirit*. Albany: State University of New York Press, 1985.

———. *James Joyce and the Philosophers at Finnegans Wake*. Evanston: Northwestern University Press, 2016.

———. *Knowledge of Things Human and Divine: Vico's New Science and "Finnegans Wake."* New Haven: Yale University Press, 2003.

Bibliography

———. *The New Art of Autobiography: An Essay on the Life of Giambattista Vico Written by Himself.* Oxford: Clarendon, 1991.

———. *Philosophy and the Return to Self-Knowledge.* New Haven: Yale University Press, 1997.

———. *Vico's New Science: A Philosophical Commentary.* Ithaca: Cornell University Press, 2015.

Verlaine, Paul. "Il pleure dans mon coeur." In *An Anthology of French Poetry from Nerval to Valery*, edited by Angel Flores, 342–43. New York: Doubleday Anchor, 1958.

Vico, Giambattista. *The New Science of Giambattista Vico.* Translated by Thomas Goddard Bergin and Max Harold Fisch. Ithaca: Cornell University Press, 1984.

———. *Vici Vindiciae.* In *Giambattista Vico: Keys to the New Science; Translations, Commentaries, and Essays*, edited by Thora Ilin Bayer and Donald Phillip Verene, 107–35. Ithaca: Cornell University Press, 2009.

Virgil. *Aeneid.* Translated by H. Rushton Fairclough. Cambridge: Harvard University Press, 1999.

von Saaz, Johannes. *The Plowman from Bohemia.* Translated by Alexander and Elizabeth Henderson. New York: Ungar, 1966.

Whitehead, A. N. *The Aims of Education and Other Essays.* New York: Free Press, 1957.

Willeford, William. *The Fool and His Scepter: A Study of Clowns and Jesters and Their Audience.* Evanston: Northwestern University Press, 1969.

Zijderveld, Anton C. *Reality in a Looking-Glass: Rationality Through an Analysis of Traditional Folly.* London: Routledge and Kegan Paul, 1982.

Index

Achilles, 4, 29, 47–49, 77
Aeacus, 29
Aesop, 40
Agrippa of Nettesheim, 71
Alcibiades, 12–13
Alembert, Jean Le Rond d', 33
Alexander the Great, 44
Anaxagoras, 61
Aquinas, Thomas, Saint, 64–67, 69
Aristotle, 28–29, 31, 48, 108, 112
    and Aquinas, 66–67
    in *Finnegans Wake*, 61
    and Homer, 9, 25, 32, 49
    on myth and metaphysics, 5–6,
        8–10, 16–18, 57
Asclepius, 14
Athena, 29, 45
Atropos, 23
Augustine, Saint, 31, 53
Ausonius, 117
Austin, J. L., 78–79

Bacon, Francis, 23, 50
Bayle, Pierre, 33
Beatrice, 29, 63
Beckett, Samuel, 65, 74–76, 79, 100
Berhnardi, A. F. 112
Berkeley, George, 55–56
Berlin, Isaiah, 39
Bloom, Harold, 33, 110
Bodin, Jean, 33
Borges, Jorge Luis, 37–58, 74, 76
Bradley, F. H., 56
Brant, Sebastian, 103–27
Browne, Thomas, 53

Bruni, Leonardo, 19, 30–31, 34
Bruno, Giordano, 64, 69–72, 75
Brutus, 29
Butler, Samuel, 40

Caesar, 29
Cantor, Georg, 52
Capasso, Nicola, 41
Carlyle, Thomas, 40
Cassirer, Ernst, 5–6, 13, 88
Cassius, 29
Cebes, 15, 50, 57
Censorinus, 37
Ceres, 48
Chou, Duke of, 25
Cicero, 19, 31, 44
Clio, 32
Clotho, 23
Collingwood, R. G., 1
Colum, Padraic, 73, 86
Confucius, 26
Crito, 8, 14, 18
Croce, Benedetto, 39
Curran, Constantine, 70
Cuzzi, Paolo, 70

Dante, 26, 29, 34, 39
    in *Finnegans Wake*, 61, 85
    Machiavelli on, 20
    Vico on, 21–22, 54, 65
Delphic oracle, 15, 23
Democritus, 31
Descartes, René, 115–17, 123
Dewey, John, 20
Diderot, Denis, 33

Index

Diocletian, 43
Diodorus Siculus, 37
Diogenes the Cynic, 105
Dionysus, 13
Dorp, Maarten van, 122
Dürer, Albrecht, 118

Eastman, George, 93
Eliot, T. S., 100
Ellul, Jacques, 97–98
Empedocles, 10, 32
Epicurus, 53
Erasmus, Desiderius, 33, 104, 119–22

Faulkner, William, 33
Faust, 23, 29
Findlay, John, 109, 111
Fornaciari, Raffaello, 70
Foucault, Michel, 112
Frith, Isabella, 70
Frost, Robert, 81
Fu Hsi, 25

Gervais, Terence White, 60
Ghezzi, Charles, S. J., 69
Giannone, Pietro, 65
Gillet, Louis, 62
Gladstone, W. E., 61
Goethe, J. W. von, 20, 23, 29, 34, 39, 61
Gorgias, 8
Guicciardini, Francesco, 51

Ham, 88
Hamlet, 22
Harrington, Sir John, 80
Hector, 29
Hegel, G. W. F., 18, 34, 39, 103
  on dialectic, 16, 24
  on Homer, 20
  on inverted world, 109–10
  on irony, 13
  Phenomenology of Spirit, 109–17
Hemingway, Ernest, 82–83
Hercules, 31
Hesiod, 4, 9
Hölderlin, Friedrich, 5
Homer, 4, 65
  Aristotle's view of, 9, 25, 32, 49
  Borges' view of, 38–39, 42, 44–50
  and Plato, 10–11
  St. Louis Hegelians' view of, 20–21, 34
Horace
  on folly, 104
  on nature of poetry, 9, 15–16, 29, 46
  Sandburg's gloss on, 87
  Vico's view of, 50
Hume, David, 53

Japeth, 88
James, William, 20
Jerome, Saint, 31
Jesus, 75, 118
John the Baptist, Saint, 71
Johnson, Lyndon, 85
Joyce, James, 40, 59–80, 82–85, 87, 91
Joyce, Nora, 60
Jove, 37, 48, 77

Kant, Immanuel, 65, 122–24
Keats, John, 5
Kooser, Ted, 81
Kristensen, Tom, 60

Lachesis, 22
Lactantius Firmianus, 31, 37
Leviathan, 92
Lincoln, Abraham, 82
Livius Andronicus, 37
Locher, Jacob, 103
Longinus, 18–19

Machiavelli, Niccolò, 19–20, 50, 61
McIntyre, J. Lewis, 70
MacLeish, Archibald, 15, 85
Malatesta, Lady Battista, 30
Malinowski, Bronislaw, 4
Mallarmé, Stéphane, 40, 110
Marcus Aurelius, 54
Marx, Groucho, 108
Matthew, 75
Menippus, 105
Mephistopheles, 29
Mercanton, Jacques, 60, 62–63
Michelet, Jules, 73, 75
Murrow, Edward R., 82

Index

Muses, 23, 69, 91
  Hesiod's view of, 4, 9, 32, 55
  Homer's use of, 21

Napoleon Bonaparte, 61
Newton, Isaac, 4
Nicolai, C. F., 112
Nietzsche, Friedrich, 27, 51, 53, 65
Noah, 88

Ockham, William of, 38
Odysseus, 4, 21, 23, 44, 47, 49
O'Hanlon, John, 79
Ovid, 20

Paracelsus, 71
Parmenides, 10
Parnell, Charles Stewart, 61
Peleus, 29
Peter, 75, 118
Petrarca, Francesco, 20
Pico della Mirandola, Giovanni, 19
Pindar, 42
Plato, 15, 21, 25–26, 31, 33–34, 55
  Borges' view of, 57
  "Plato's year," 53–54
  quarrel with poets, 8–11
  and self-knowledge, 39
Plutarch, 8, 58
Pluto, 47–48
Pompey, 29
Pope, Alexander, 41–42, 46
Proserpine, 48
Ptolemy, 43

Quinet, Edgar, 75
Quintilian, 12, 19

Rabelais, François, 105
Rimbaud, Arthur, 30, 110
Rose, Danis, 79
Rosenkranz, Karl, 112
Rousseau, Jean-Jacques, 73
Royce, Josiah, 53
Russell, Bertrand, 53

Saaz, Johannes von, 113
Sandburg, Carl, 81–102

Sandburg, Paula, 81
Santayana, George, 83
Schliemann, Heinrich, 29
Schopenhauer, Arthur, 54, 65
Scotus, Duns, 68
Seneca, 31
Shakespeare, William, 20, 22, 26, 31, 34, 61, 110
Shem, 88
Sigismund August II, 107
Silenus, 12–13
Simmias, 57
Simonides, 8
Snider, Denton, 20
Socrates, 5, 8
  Brant's view of, 117, 119
  Socratic irony, 40
  Socratic method, 12–15, 17
  view of death, 21, 50, 57, 68
Solla, Nicola, 41
Solomon, 40, 50–51, 106
Spengler, Oswald, 34
Sphinx, 93–94
Steichen, Edward, 85
Steinbeck, John, 82
Straumann, Heinrich, 63, 73
Swift, Jonathan, 107

Theophrastus, 31
Thetis, 29
Thrasymachus, 12
Tieck, Ludwig, 112–13
Tindall, William York, 65
Typhon, 28

Ulysses. *See* Odysseus
Usener, Hermann, 6

Valletta, Giuseppe, 41
Van Doren, Mark, 85
Varro, Marcus Terentius, 31
Velázquez, Diego, 53
Verlaine, Paul, 30
Vettori, Francesco, 19
Vico, Giambattista, 19
  and Borges, 37–39, 41–42, 48–50, 55
  in *Finnegans Wake*, 65, 69–77
  view of Dante, 21–22, 54

Index

Virgil, 24, 63
Voltaire, 33, 107

Warren, Earl, 85
Weaver, Harriet Shaw, 61, 71, 73
Wên, King, 25
Whitehead, A. N., 27

Whitman, Walt, 81–82, 100
Wilhelm, Richard, 25
Wordsworth, William, 4

Zeydel, Edwin, 118
Zijderveld, Anton C., 108–9

www.ingramcontent.com/pod-product-compliance
Lightning Source LLC
Chambersburg PA
CBHW031501160426
43195CB00010BB/1063